"As someone who is passionate about helping organizations be more neuroinclusive, I especially appreciate that Rachel Radway has offered actionable tools for people leaders and HR professionals. The information on various ways people can give or receive feedback and offer clarity in communication is especially useful."

—Pasha Marlowe, LMFT, CEO of Neurobelonging, speaker, and author of *Creating Cultures of Neuroinclusion: A Framework for Peopling and Engaging Neurodiverse Talent*

"I resonate with almost every single word Rachel Radway's written in *Perceptive*. Today, I realize that my sensitivity is a gift. It's given me so much information that I haven't listened to as often as I should have, but I do now. This book is necessary reading for everyone who has been told, 'You're being too sensitive. Get over it. Leaders don't cry.' *Perceptive* will validate so many, and in the process help people realize they are not crazy, and they are not alone. Thank you for writing a book that fights the stereotypes that so many of us have fought against. I can't wait to read more!"

—Donna Star, president of DStar Coaching and Consulting and author of *Unsuccessfully Successful*

"*Perceptive* is an insightful exploration of how appreciating neurodiversity benefits both individuals and teams. It offers leaders a blueprint for understanding that our differences should not be obstacles, but the very source of breakthrough innovation and high performance."

—Ed Thompson, founder & CEO of Uptimize and author of *A Hidden Force: Unlocking the Potential of Neurodiversity at Work*

"For everyone who's been told they're too sensitive, Rachel Radway's *Perceptive* offers a compelling invitation to recognize our strengths and own our power as boldly empathetic, authentic, and inclusive leaders."

—Minette Norman, award-winning author of *The Boldly Inclusive Leader*

"*Perceptive* is about people who notice more, feel more, think more. Many have felt different or even flawed. But being wired differently can be your biggest advantage, as Rachel Radway shows. Reading this book will make you more aware of your unique talents!"

—Esther Bergsma, expert on high sensitivity and author of *The Brain of the Highly Sensitive Person*

"In *Perceptive*, Rachel Radway draws on personal experience and intimate conversations with highly sensitive leaders to help readers embrace their different wiring as a source of strength. If you struggle navigating a world built for less sensitive minds, *Perceptive* invites you to redefine your path toward fulfillment."

—Ludmila Praslova, PhD, SHRM-SCP, professor, Organizational Psychology & Business, VUSC, and award-winning author of *The Canary Code: A Guide to Neurodiversity, Dignity, and Intersectional Belonging at Work*

"*Perceptive* is a heartfelt invitation to reconsider how we understand sensory sensitivity in neurodivergent women and shines a spotlight on the growing conversation around the impact of late-discovered autistic identity."

—Melanie Deziel, autistic author, speaker, and creator of *The Late Diagnosed Diaries*

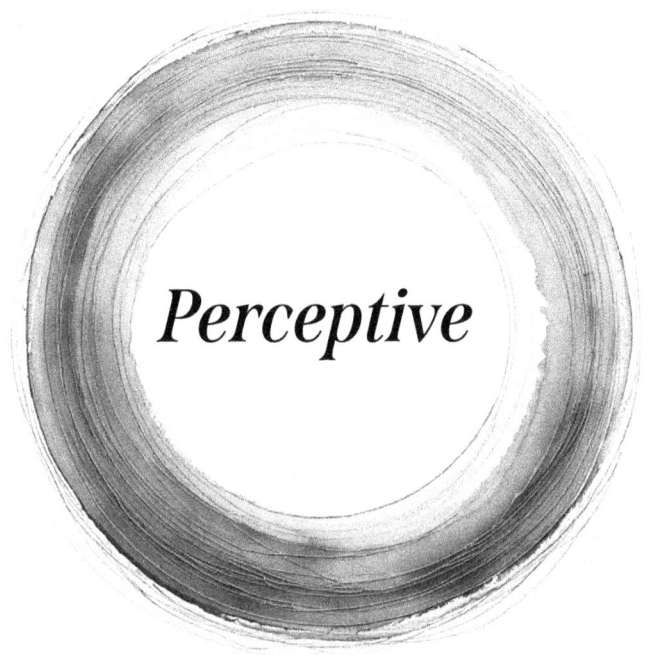

Perceptive

Insights for leaders who
feel more, process deeply,
and think differently

Rachel Eve Radway

Copyright © 2025 by Rachel Eve Radway

All rights reserved. No part of this book may be reproduced or retransmitted in any form or by any means without the written permission of the publisher.

ISBN 979-8-9928391-0-4 (print)
ISBN 979-8-9928391-1-1 (ebook)

Seaglass Books
https://www.rercoaching.com/
info@rercoaching.com

Production Management: Weaving Influence, Inc.
Cover and Interior Design: Rachel Royer
Copyediting: Meredith Mix
Typesetting: Lori Weidert
Proofreading: Keri Hales

Printed in the United States of America

To all my G.R.I.T. Collaborative members past, present, and future: Give yourselves grace and trust. Resilience and intuition are already yours.

Contents

Introduction ix
   A note on structure xvii

1 What is high sensory perception? 1
   A note on language 3
   Shy, anxious, or introverted? 5
   The brain science, oversimplified 6
   The sensory continuum and the mixing
      board metaphor 7
   Sensation seekers and high sensitivity 8
   Empaths 9
   Coming full circle 12
   Takeaways 14

2 Neurodiversity and neurodivergence 15
   What's in a name? 19
   Can you be both an HSP and autistic? 27
   Takeaways 32

3	**Empathy and its darker side**	33
	People-pleasing and the struggle to say no	36
	Boundaries aren't just to keep people out	38
	Takeaways	45
4	**Connecting the dots**	47
	Strategic thinking: Seeing both the big picture and the details	50
	Intuition and trust	53
	Takeaways	61
5	**Highly perceptive in the workplace**	63
	Speed vs. diligence	64
	Small talk and being social at work	66
	Physical environments	69
	Office politics	72
	Toxic environments	72
	Solutions that benefit everyone	76
	To disclose or not to disclose?	78
	Takeaways	79
6	**The highly perceptive leader**	81
	More struggles and strengths of highly perceptive women leaders	86
	More keys to success	94
	Takeaways	96
7	**Burnout**	97
	Masking and burnout	100
	The costs of masking	102
	Lack of self-awareness and burnout	105

Neurodivergent burnout 106
What are the signs of neurodivergent burnout? 109
Takeaways... 111

8 Redefining self-care 113
Get more, and better, sleep.. 116
Eat when you need to.. 119
Get outside 120
Practice calendar care 121
Take a sound bath 123
Protect your energy 124
Find your micro-moments of joy............................... 125
Ask for what you want and what you need 127
Find your community 129
Takeaways... 132

Conclusion... 133
What do you want your life to look like?.................... 138
Giving ourselves grace 141

Reflection questions 143

Endnotes.. 147

Resources 155

Acknowledgments 161

About the Author 165

About RER Coaching 167

Introduction

I was so burned out that I had to quit my job, sell my condo, and move to rural Peru to find the time and space I needed to recover.

Or start to, anyway. It took years to recover fully, which says something about how much damage I'd done to myself.

As the director of a team that spanned 17 time zones in the tech division of a Fortune 500, I sometimes felt like I worked around the clock. I definitely didn't understand the concept of boundaries back then.

I'd always been a hard worker and a high achiever and had high expectations of myself and others. Still more work to do at 7 p.m.? I'd just keep going. Eat dinner at my desk, go home, go to bed because I didn't have the time or energy to do anything else, get up the next day, rinse and repeat.

In the open-plan office, I found it hard to focus given the constant noise, microwaved-meal smells, temperatures that varied between freezing and hot, harsh artificial lighting, and other distractions. It was hard for me to be productive during the workday anyway, because I was usually running—sometimes literally—

from one meeting to the next. Which is why there was always so much work still to do at 7 p.m. But, I rationalized, it was quiet then. Everyone else had left the building.

I felt frustrated that it seemed so easy for my colleagues to do their jobs and then go out or go home, leave work behind, and have a life. I didn't know how they were able to do that.

The work environment had become toxic, which depleted me even more. I was trying to manage not only my own challenges and frustrations but those of my team members and peers too; I couldn't help taking it all on emotionally and energetically. Some of us wanted to make big changes (to the culture and the product) but felt powerless in the face of the entrenched bureaucracy and internal politics. The negativity weighed heavily on me, and I didn't handle it well.

It wasn't the first time in my career that I'd struggled with some of these things. It wasn't even the second or third. But I finally reached my limit that year, in that job.

The burnout showed up in a few ways, but I'm not sure I recognized the extent or severity of it then. I was physically exhausted and dealing with chronic pain. I had periods of brain fog. The most noticeable symptom to me now, although I didn't realize it at the time, was the change in my personality. I used to laugh a lot at work and enjoy the people I worked with. I used to love leading a team and supporting others' growth and development.

By then, though, I'd stopped laughing. I was impatient. I wasn't particularly empathetic. I tried to be "professional" in my interactions, but with a couple of close colleagues I felt safe with, I let the resentment, bitterness, and sarcasm out. I'd become someone I didn't like very much.

When I resigned, my VP and SVP, the head of the business unit, both warmly invited me to return if I should change my mind, so I was reassured that my evil alter ego hadn't done as much harm as she could have. But I probably left just in time.

Looking back, I have so much empathy and compassion for the person I was then. Knowing what I do now, understanding a lot more about myself and the way I'm wired, it all makes sense. The lifelong patterns that showed up in school and work situations and in personal relationships that left me sad, frustrated and sometimes ashamed, now had context.

The restlessness and searching that led me not only to leave numerous jobs but also to set what must be world records for moving house—as of the time of writing, I've lived in nine countries, eight US states and countless towns and cities within them, for a total of 50+ moves—all make sense now.

What do I know now that I didn't when I was struggling? That my brain is wired a little differently from what society considers "typical."(Actually, I *had* known some of it then—I'd just forgotten. I've learned a lot more since.) More about this later. I'll start by saying that I have a little-known trait I call *high sensory perception*.

You may have heard of this trait under a different name. In the late 1990s, a psychologist named Elaine Aron published a book called *The Highly Sensitive Person* (Broadway Books, 1997). She described a group of people with a set of characteristics that's now been identified in several species besides humans (there are highly sensitive cats, dogs, and many others). There's even a scientific name for it: *sensory processing sensitivity* (SPS; not to be confused with *sensory processing disorder*, a treatable disorder usually diagnosed in early childhood).

The book was a revelation to me when I read it, a few years after it came out. It explained so much about the way my brain worked and why I often responded differently to things than others around me did. I filed the information away—and then forgot about it.

I believe we learn things when we're ready for them, and apparently, I wasn't ready then for the changes that came when I reread the book more than 20 years later.

This rediscovery was sparked by a series of events that happened shortly after I launched my coaching business. I was working with women leaders, and although each client came to our coaching engagement with her own goals and challenges, there were many similar themes. When I reread Aron's book and truly integrated what I learned, I started connecting the dots. And connecting dots is something highly sensitive people do a lot.

As I read more about the trait, conducted my own market research, and coached more clients, two things became clear: (1) Most of the clients who found me early on, before I'd decided where I wanted to specialize, were also highly sensitive (even though many of them weren't familiar with the term or Aron's work); and (2) not only did I want to work with these women, most of whom were facing challenges that I understood and empathized with from my own experience, but I wanted to go a step further. Once these bright, talented, high-achieving leaders were thriving themselves, they'd be in ideal positions to help cultivate psychologically safer and more inclusive workplaces, something I'm deeply committed to.

I'd found my purpose and my people. There was just one problem.

"Sensitive" is a bad word in our society. Even worse in the tech industry's "work hard, play hard" culture. Anyone who grew up being told, "You're too sensitive," or "You shouldn't take everything so personally," instinctively knew as they entered the workforce—if not earlier—that being seen as sensitive probably wouldn't do them any favors in their career. The stigma's real and powerful.

In an informal poll conducted on my personal Facebook page, I asked what came to mind when folks heard the term "highly sensitive" as it relates to a person.

A few of the responses I got:

> "Difficult, high maintenance, on the spectrum, and we need to be very mindful of what we say or do around [them] to avoid triggering them."

> "Insecurity issues."

> "Strongly negative impression, difficult to work with, easily offended."

> "Too easily upset."

My Facebook profile page, unlike my business page, is private, and I only connect there with people I know and who know me. Every response above was from an educated person raised in a progressive, urban environment—people who are fairly savvy about unconscious bias.

I don't have to imagine what might come up were I to ask the same question in a less open-minded environment—or the effects the comments might have on people who grew up hearing them.

One leader I spoke with this for this book shared with me that as a child she was always being told, "You're crying? I'll give you something to cry about." When I asked what challenges she faces at work now because of her sensitivity, the first thing she said was, "Trying to do a really good job of masking any emotion. That's something that I'm always trying to do."

In researching for this book, I spoke with women leaders in different roles, functions, and industries, from a variety of backgrounds, ranging in age from their 30s to their 70s. And while I wish I could say that we've come a long way as a society in our understanding and acceptance of diversity in all its forms, some of the most disturbing accounts are recent and involve people in executive and other leadership roles who need to do much, much better.

I asked an HR leader, who couldn't give details for confidentiality reasons, whether she'd witnessed any bias, discrimination or derogatory remarks made toward or about anyone on the basis of perceived sensitivity. Her response: "Oh, for sure. Especially behind closed doors when people are talking about leadership, when people are talking about performance, when they're talking about collaboration and someone's ability to function across teams. This concept of being hypersensitive or difficult comes up. It happens. Yeah, it happens pretty frequently, actually."

Think about the implications for candidates interviewing for jobs. For stellar performers who meet or exceed all their KPIs and OKRs but are denied promotion after promotion because they're wired a little differently.

This impacts us all.

The toxic environment I described at the beginning of this introduction wasn't the first I'd encountered, nor, unfortunately, the last. I launched my coaching business after more than 25 years in the corporate world. I held leadership roles in content strategy and development, brand management, communications, operations, and then design operations, in companies ranging from tiny tech startups to national nonprofits to huge global enterprises. I worked in aerospace, public policy, consumer software and SaaS, e-commerce, edtech, fintech, and more, in three different countries.

All this experience is what's made me so passionate about making workplaces better places to work. And it's why I'm writing this book: to raise awareness of this lesser-known, but fairly common, form of diversity—neurodiversity, in fact—and to start changing the narrative around sensitivity and neurodivergence.

Awareness is key, both for those who have the traits I describe and may have struggled because of them, and for anyone in a position to make decisions that affect people in the workplace. That is, just about everyone.

Because not only is it *not* a weakness or a fault or something to be masked, heightened sensitivity is actually a set of superpowers. You'll learn in the first few chapters why highly sensitive = highly perceptive, and perceptiveness is, inarguably, a valuable asset in leaders of organizations and in society in general.

I've been talking with people and writing posts and newsletters about this topic for quite a while now. Some readers are courageous enough to raise their hands and say yes, this is me, more of this, please. Some of the messages that touch me the most deeply, though, are the private ones, saying things like "I feel like you've been inside my head. I didn't know about this and want to know more. Thank you for sharing this—now I know I'm not crazy or broken."

This book is for everyone who grew up hearing, "You're too sensitive," or was told to grow a thicker skin. For everyone who's wondered why they seem to pick up more than others do, or read people better, or see several steps ahead, and felt that they might be wired just a little bit differently. For the bright, talented, high achievers with high standards for themselves and others, who don't like the rules as they're currently laid out. My hope is that you'll see some of yourself reflected here and learn more about your strengths and how to leverage them. Maybe, too, learn some tools and techniques to help better manage some of the challenges that come with being highly perceptive—there are always two sides of the coin!

Most importantly, know that you're not crazy, you're not broken, and you're not alone.

This book is also for inclusive leaders, HR/People/Talent/Culture/DEIBAJ professionals (the most inclusive version of this acronym stands for diversity, equity, inclusion, belonging, accessibility, and justice), and anyone who manages a team of more than two people. As up to 30 percent of the global population is thought to be highly sensitive—highly perceptive—you're probably interacting with, managing, and maybe even reporting to someone with this trait every day. You might not recognize it; they might not want you to. But I guarantee that some of the best and brightest in your organization are highly perceptive, and when they're in an environment where they feel safe and free to be themselves and bring all their gifts to light, everyone will benefit.

It's beyond time that this gift is acknowledged and shared with the world.

A note on structure

Although not formally organized into sections, the book's contents fall into four different parts:

> Chapters 1 and 2 are about heightened sensitivity, associated traits, and how our brains are wired differently.
>
> Chapters 3 and 4 highlight a few specific characteristics of highly perceptive people—the strengths and the struggles.
>
> Chapters 5 and 6 focus on how these traits—both the superpowers and the drawbacks—can manifest in the workplace and in leadership.
>
> Chapters 7 and 8 look at burnout, why highly perceptive people might be more susceptible to it, and how to prevent it.

There's no right way to read the book. If you're newer to these topics, though, I recommend starting with Chapters 1 and 2 and then skipping to whatever piques your interest.

What is high sensory perception?

"Wasn't it amazing how, when Dad came home and you could hear how he closed the truck door or how he was walking on the ground, you knew whether you could stay in the house or should run out the back door?"

Karen Renee Halseth, an intuitive business coach, was talking with two of her siblings many years ago, when their mother was passing. As she relived this vivid childhood memory with them—describing the state of suspense she existed in every day after school for years, waiting for a sign of their volatile father's mood—they looked at her blankly. They had no idea what she was talking about.

And yet she knows how critical this sensitivity to her environment was for her. She had to make a split-second decision every day: Take a chance and stay home or seek safety at a neighbor's or friend's house. Her perceptiveness, as she said, "was absolute radar and it probably kept me alive."

At the same time, Karen Renee grew up hearing, "You're too sensitive. You need to grow a thicker skin."

I can relate; I was told the same thing, and I've heard it from many other highly perceptive people. As children, the world sometimes (or often) felt like too much for us. We felt too much. We heard or saw or experienced too much.

We got the message that *we* were too much.

"I just thought I needed to tone myself down," said Karen Renee, "because my friends didn't react to things the way I did. I thought if only I could learn how to manage this, then maybe I wouldn't feel so much."

What does a bright, observant, sensitive child do with that?

Young Karen Renee, in her words, "became a watcher. I would watch my friends with their parents and see, 'Oh, that gets positive reinforcement. Be like that.' Or, 'don't be like *that*.' So I created a persona that worked really well in the world and left me feeling very lonely and empty inside."

I've heard so many versions of this heartbreaking story from smart, talented, successful women—corporate leaders, entrepreneurs and business owners, internationally recognized speakers and published authors, artists, musicians, and creatives of all kinds.

Although I wasn't afraid for my physical safety growing up, I was a watcher too. A highly perceptive child, I knew I was different from an early age, and while I didn't do it consciously intending to adopt their behaviors, I observed other kids and adults. And I picked up a lot more information than I realized.

This isn't all that unusual. An estimated 30 percent of the global population is born highly sensitive.[1]

A note on language

I use a number of terms throughout this book to refer to a constellation of traits that a large segment of the global population shares. The terms aren't truly interchangeable, but I sometimes use them that way. In some cases, it's simply to avoid repetition. In others, it's an intentional reframe to a neutral or positive term from one with negative connotations.

I use *high sensitivity* or *highly sensitive* mainly in the early chapters, to set the stage. These are the terms most people are familiar with—even though they are frequently misunderstood and stigmatized.

Environmental sensitivity (ES) is another term for high or heightened sensitivity. *Sensory processing sensitivity* (SPS) is the scientific term for the trait.

Perceptive is defined variously by Merriam-Webster and Cambridge online dictionaries as:

- responsive to sensory stimuli: discerning
- capable of or exhibiting keen perception: observant
- characterized by sympathetic understanding or insight
- very good at noticing and understanding things that many people do not notice

Each of these applies to the population Elaine Aron refers to as highly sensitive, and the people I describe in this book. When I use these terms, people who've been socialized to think of sensitivity as a weakness get excited. They start to see their characteristics and patterns they've thought of as problems in the past in a much more positive light.

High sensory perception is a term I use to tie together the physical, emotional, and energetic aspects of this constellation of traits. *Sensitivity,* in contrast, is often thought of in a specific context—sensitivity to heat or light, for example, or emotional sensitivity. While everyone is different, people who score high on sensitivity assessments tend to be responsive to many different kinds of stimuli. I go into more detail later in this chapter.

Handily, high sensory perception can also be shortened to HSP, the broadly used acronym for "highly sensitive person." I use HSP to refer to people, mostly because there's no widely recognized acronym for "highly perceptive person"—yet!

Wired differently is, admittedly, vague. It's also the most accurate and the most inclusive. Each of our brains works a little differently from everyone else's, so, technically, this language applies to everyone. Some of us are wired a little more differently than others, though, which I go into more in the next chapter.

Shy, anxious, or introverted?

Sensitive children are often labeled shy or sometimes difficult. Sensitive adults might be called reserved or assumed to have social anxiety. In fact, someone can be all of these things and not be highly sensitive, or vice versa—be highly sensitive and have none of these other qualities.

High sensitivity is also sometimes confused with introversion, another personality trait that's distinct from shyness. While there is a fair amount of overlap between sensitivity and introversion, and Elaine Aron's research showed that 70 percent of highly sensitive people (HSPs) are introverts,[2] there are introverts who aren't highly sensitive and HSPs (30 percent!) who are extraverts.

The definitions of introversion and extraversion that resonate with me center on how someone recharges—where they get their energy. By these definitions, introverts recharge by being on their own, and extraverts are energized by social interaction. This doesn't mean that introverts are necessarily antisocial or natural loners (although some are); we (I'm an introvert) simply need more alone time than others and may prefer to spend time one to one or in small groups, rather than with a lot of people at once.

A distinction that Jenn Turnham, extraverted HSP and coach based in Western Australia, makes between introverts and extraverts is that the former process their information internally, and think before they speak. Extraverts, according to Jenn, "need to speak in order to think."[3]

Life can be confusing for extraverted HSPs until they understand that they're wired differently. They tend to be very social and outgoing—but sense that they're not like other extraverts. They need more down time, more recharging time, and can sometimes feel conflicted about wanting to go out and be with others versus needing rest or quiet.

It's not surprising that they might feel confused or conflicted. If HSPs are about 30 percent of the population and 30 percent of those are extraverts, then only 9 percent are both; these folks may not meet a lot of other people like themselves.

The brain science, oversimplified

The human brain can process about 11 million pieces of information in one second, unconsciously. The estimate for how much most of us process consciously in that second: about 40–50 pieces.[4]

That's a lot of information that most brains are filtering out.

A very oversimplified explanation for high sensory perception (high sensitivity) is that our brains are taking in *more* of that incoming information—that is, filtering out *less*—and processing the information we take in more deeply.

In other words, our brains are *more* active *more* of the time.

There's an excellent book, *The Brain of the Highly Sensitive Person* (Booklight Publishing, 2020), by HSP expert and social science researcher Esther Bergsma, that I highly recommend for anyone interested in the science underlying the trait. Bergsma cites various functional MRI and other studies that have shown different regions in the brain are activated in HSPs for specific tasks, and that more connections show up between various areas of the brain in HSPs. In a recent YouTube video,[5] she also mentions EEGs and Diffusion Tensor Imaging (DTI) studies that have shown differences in the strength of certain brain waves in

HSPs, and that the microstructure of HSP brains looks different from that of non-highly sensitive brains.

What does all that mean?

That we really are perceiving more environmental stimuli, such as sounds, subtle differences in temperature or light, scents, tastes, textures, and more, and may perceive them more quickly than people around us. And we're picking up more energetic and emotional signals from our surroundings—this is how so many of us can read a room or easily understand nonverbal communication.

It also means that there's nothing wrong with us—we're not broken or crazy. We're simply picking up on things that other people aren't.

Processing all this data more deeply includes what Elaine Aron calls our "pause-to-check" system. Naturally, processing more information more deeply takes the brain more time. Many high-sensory folks may stay on the periphery of a new group of people observing the energy, interactions, and group dynamics before deciding how to join in. Others may hesitate to jump into an animated discussion because they want to carefully process everything that's being said and respond in a meaningful way. Too often, highly perceptive people are judged or criticized for being too slow or reserved, when they're actually processing a lot more of what's going on than their critics are and being thoughtful about how to contribute.

The sensory continuum and the mixing board metaphor

Everyone is sensitive to certain things at certain times. I've noticed that hormonal cycles and sleep patterns affect my own sensitivity levels and pain threshold, and this seems to be backed up by research.[6,7] Trauma can cause heightened sensitivity to stimuli, too.

I envision the universe of sensitivities as a huge sound mixing board, with rows of channels that can be dialed up (high sensitivity) or down (low sensitivity). The channel labels include all kinds of stimuli and substances I've already mentioned: sounds, scents/smells, light, color, textures, alcohol, caffeine, and many more.

Everyone has at least one or two channels that are dialed up. The more channels you have higher in the up position, the more sensitive you are. The research team behind the site sensitivity research.com refers to a sensitivity continuum. About 30 percent of the population falls on the high end of the continuum, 30 percent on the low end, and 40 percent in the middle—a fairly flat bell curve.[8]

The research site, which defines sensitive people simply as "those who are more strongly affected by what they experience," explains that sensitivity is partially caused by genetic and neurobiological differences, and is an "established, recognised, and empirically verified human trait."[9]

Sensation seekers and high sensitivity

Another human personality trait that can cause confusion in high-sensory people is sensation seeking, "characterized by the seeking of novel and intense experiences."[10] This trait, like extraversion, might seem at odds with the preferences of many HSPs, who are often thought of as shy, quiet types who stay at home and avoid excitement of any kind.

In all the HSP self-assessments I've taken, I score just about as highly as possible. And most of the time these days, given the choice between going out to a party or event and curling up at home with a good book or movie, my sofa will win, hands down.

That said, I've traveled all over the world. I've chosen to live in eight countries outside the US, crisscrossing the globe a few times. I've moved *a lot*. I've flown in helicopters, twin-seater Cessnas, and hot air balloons, and piloted a glider. Paraglided off a cliff in New Zealand and rode many miles in the flatbed of a very old truck in Tibet to view Chomolungma (the local name for Mt. Everest). I love riding on the back of motorcycles.

I've experimented with all kinds of hobbies and foods and hairstyles and hair colors (and I'm not talking about subtly elegant highlights, here; I once had extensions all the way down my back that ranged from walnut to mahogany to platinum blonde—all braided together—and, for another memorable period, dyed my hair Bozo-the-clown red).

I've always sought out my own version of novel and intense experiences.

As Elaine Aron and her colleagues found in research published in 2023,[11] SPS and sensation seeking are unrelated traits, and it's very possible to have both, as I do.

Empaths

Another category that deserves a mention here is that of empaths. Anita Moorjani, in her 2021 book *Sensitive is the New Strong*, defines an empath as "a highly sensitive person who feels and absorbs the thoughts, emotions, and energy of others."[12]

Just as HSPs can be sensitive to different things and no two have exactly the same "mixing board pattern," empaths, too, can be sensitive in different ways. I've spoken with several empaths who don't have challenges with sounds or smells or textures the way I do, for example.

In addition to thoughts, emotions, and energy, some empaths—often referred to as physical empaths[13]—can also pick up pain and physical sensations from other people. An empath who hasn't yet learned this or how to manage it might feel a headache or nausea or a collection of physical sensations when they're in a crowded place—and then realize that those sensations vanish as soon as they leave that crowded environment.

There are people who believe that empaths and HSPs are completely separate; I disagree. I think it's just a question of which channels are dialed up on the mixing board.

Reading Moorjani's book, memories came flooding back from my early 20s. I lived in San Francisco, and, since I didn't drive or have a car then, I took MUNI, the city's extensive bus and light-rail network, everywhere. One of the routes I rode frequently, the 22 Fillmore, is notable for the diversity of the neighborhoods it serves. On my rides, I passed through the Marina and Pacific Heights, some of the wealthiest areas in the city, and several other neighborhoods with plenty of character (and characters), and ended up in what was then one of the most dangerous parts of the Mission District. (I volunteered there. I'll never forget the morning after one of my volunteer stints, when I saw on the news that two people had been shot the night before at the same corner where I'd been waiting for the bus about 15 minutes earlier.)

What I remember most about those rides is that I rarely ended up sitting alone. Inevitably, whenever anyone with a visible or audible mental illness boarded the bus, they beelined for the seat next to me. I was some sort of magnet.

It was frightening, for a lot of reasons. I knew a lot less about mental illness then than I do now, for one thing. I didn't know if they might be dangerous. A lot of these people were homeless. Many didn't have regular access to showers or clean clothes. A lot of them shouted. I got easily overwhelmed by the odors and the loud noise. More frightening was that I had no idea why they were always drawn to *me*, or what to do about it.

One day, a well-known psychic, the late Victoria Bullis, joined San Francisco's popular KFOG morning show, which I listened to regularly. She answered callers' questions about all kinds of interesting things, seemingly accurately. I decided to make an appointment with her for a reading.

On the day of my appointment, when I finally arrived at her office after almost an hour on two different bus lines, Victoria looked at me and then did a double take. She asked if I'd driven there, and when I said I'd taken buses, shook her head. She told me I was an empath, that I'd collected all sorts of energies that didn't belong to me, and that my aura was really muddy. She asked permission to clear it all out, and when she'd finished, showed me a way to prevent this from happening again: a common technique I've now learned variations of to create a protective bubble around myself, an invisible, semipermeable membrane that lets me decide what kind of energies I allow in and out.

This was completely out of my realm of experience, and I didn't know quite what to make of it, but from what I remember, I rarely had uninvited company on the bus again. (I'll explain how to do it yourself in Chapter 8, on self-care.)

Coming full circle

When empaths and other highly perceptive people learn to create and honor their own boundaries and take care of themselves so they can take care of others, their gifts can benefit everyone around them.

When Karen Renee served as spa director as well as operations and HR manager of a large boutique hotel, her empathy and intuition earned her respect, trust, and gratitude across the organization.

An employee who worked on the grounds crew wanted to interview for a busser position in the hotel restaurant. She got to know him and asked about his background. She learned that he had a degree in psychology from a university in Mexico and that he'd studied American TV shows for years to learn English. She knew he was a hard and dedicated worker. But the restaurant manager kept refusing to interview him, believing that someone at what he considered the bottom rung of the hospitality ladder wouldn't succeed in the busser role. Karen Renee pushed the manager because she felt strongly that this employee would be an asset in the restaurant—and that the man deserved the chance. She finally pointed out that under the law he couldn't continue to refuse the man an opportunity to interview.

Years later, she returned to the hotel to run a retreat with her own clients, and not only was the employee still working there—he was now the banquet manager. Her empathy and intuition in this case benefited not only the employee but also the restaurant manager, who gained a terrific worker who quickly climbed that ladder, and all the guests who enjoyed restaurant or event service for many years afterwards.

Today in her coaching business, Karen Renee uses her "unique ability in illuminating areas that clients can't see—the hidden patterns and conditioning that influence their lives."

One example: A client who'd been a successful family law attorney for more than 20 years. At first, she'd thrived in litigation, finding it both challenging and rewarding. Over time, though, she became drained by courtroom battles. The system felt broken, and she felt disheartened and weary.

The client wore her power suit to court like armor. She often talked about the struggle of being a woman advocating for her clients' rights in a male-dominated courtroom environment that seemed to disregard heart and, ironically, fairness.

Working with Karen Renee, she became aware of how she'd disconnected from a significant part of herself—the feminine—while giving her masculine side full control to do her job. As she acknowledged this, grief surfaced, and their work together deepened. She began taking steps to bring her whole self into the courtroom.

Eventually, she completed her certification as a private judge, which allowed her to make rulings without the traditional courtroom experience. Her confidence soared, along with her desire to create a new model for couples going through divorce. Within two years, she'd achieved her dream and left litigation behind.

When she did the work and embraced her entire self—with the support, guidance and insight of her intuitive, empathic coach—every aspect of her life improved, and she flourished.

Takeaways

- ☑ Up to 30 percent of the world's population is born more responsive to physical and environmental stimuli than other people. This group also processes information more deeply than others.

- ☑ Research shows that this trait is at least partially based in genetics and neurobiology: Our brains *are* wired differently.

- ☑ High sensory perception/SPS is distinct from other traits and conditions like shyness, introversion, and social anxiety.

- ☑ Not all highly sensitive people respond to the same things.

- ☑ People can be high sensory and "sensation seekers" at the same time. These HSPs still need certain conditions to thrive, such as more down time before and after the more intense experiences they seek out.

- ☑ Empaths are highly sensitive to other people's emotions and energy and may or may not be highly sensitive to other stimuli as well. If they lack awareness or boundaries, they may take on—without realizing it—feelings or physical sensations that don't belong to them.

- ☑ Despite the messages we often receive from childhood that we need to be fixed or treated, highly perceptive, high-sensory people have incredible strengths that the world needs now more than ever.

Neurodiversity and neurodivergence

The topics of neurodiversity and neurodivergence are vast, complex, and nuanced, and I'm still early in my own journey of discovery. One of my goals in this chapter is to share my own story in case it resonates with readers the way the stories I heard and read did with me. Another is to raise awareness: both of the world of naturally occurring neurocognitive differences and of the growing numbers of people (and women in particular) who are learning that there are explanations for patterns and challenges in their lives that may have seemed inexplicable before. And, finally, that it's not about the labels. It's about understanding more about ourselves, learning to give ourselves some grace, and embracing the gifts each one of us has—as well as learning to ask for support or accommodation when we need it, without shame or embarrassment. In the Resources section at the end of the book, I've listed some of the many books, videos, and websites I've found helpful; there are plenty more, and by the time you're reading this, I'm sure available resources will have increased exponentially.

When I interviewed Kalen Cobb, a licensed social worker and therapist for Gen Z and Millennials, for this book, I asked what she thinks of when she hears the term perceptive. She laughed.

"I'm laughing because the person I'm thinking about who used to call me highly sensitive was my dear mother, who I love very much and am very close to. And I recognize that the language that she uses to describe me has moved from 'highly sensitive' to 'very perceptive.' And there is a connection there: 'You are always thinking about the world beyond just what is in front of you.'"

Kalen continued: "As a perceptive human, I always think of seeing the little grains of the world, seeing life beyond what's in front of you. I even explained it to a friend as like seeing beyond the veil. Maybe this is getting way too woo-woo, but I think, as people who are highly sensitive or who are perceptive or who are neurodivergent, we see beyond this natural world, and with the people I've connected to there's also been a spiritual dimension to some of this neurodivergence. And I think the word 'perceptive' really takes into account all of that."

There's a lot to parse here. I found it interesting that Kalen's mother has changed the way she talks about her, referring to her as perceptive, rather than highly sensitive—a nuance that shows perceptiveness in her mother, too, and an awareness of the stigma associated with high sensitivity. (I'm making an assumption—I didn't ask Kalen specifically about this because we had so many other things to talk about!)

One of the threads we did follow was her use of the term *neurodivergence*. Although neurodiversity and neurodivergence are being talked and written about fairly frequently now and have become common in some contexts, they're still not widely understood among the general population. So what do they mean?

The term *neurodiversity* is usually attributed to Australian sociologist Judy Singer, who used it in her 1998 university honors thesis, although there's some debate now[1] about whether she coined it. I'm less interested in its origins than what it means, which is essentially that there is naturally occurring variety in the way we all think, perceive, and process information—the way our brains function.

"No two brains are alike, and we are all wired differently," wrote Ed Thompson, founder and CEO of Uptimize, a neurodiversity training and consulting company, in an article in *Psychology Today*, "Why Neurodiversity Is Misunderstood in the Workplace."[2]

Which brings up a nitpicky but important point: Any organization or group of people, in any context or culture, is inherently neurodiverse, as more than one person (or brain) means there must be at least a little neurological diversity. An individual isn't described as neurodiverse but as *neurodivergent*, meaning different from "neurotypical." (And we can debate the existence of an actual neurotypical brain at some other point; I don't think I've ever met one.)

The *neurodiversity paradigm*, proposed in 2012 by author, educator, queer futurist, and psychologist Dr. Nick Walker, is a framework for understanding naturally occurring brain differences as part of a spectrum of neurocognitive function rather than a set of disorders.[3]

According to the neurodiversity paradigm, neurodivergence is simply a difference that isn't currently accommodated by society. It's similar to the social model of disability—as opposed to the medical model—which states that people are disabled only to the extent to which societal norms, structures and systems don't accommodate their individual needs. An example: Imagine that every building, residential, commercial, or institutional, was accessibly designed. Built with entrance ramps, wide doorways that open automatically or by means of an easily accessible control, spacious elevators with floor buttons that could be reached by someone of any height, wide hallways, kitchens and bathrooms with fixtures that could accommodate various support needs, etc. Imagine that every parking lot had wider spaces, and every street had broad sidewalks. Stores had built-in, automated systems to allow items on higher shelves to be easily reached. Someone who navigates this world in a wheelchair wouldn't seem disabled if they could get around and live their life as easily as someone walking on two feet. And per the neurodiversity paradigm, if our environments were more welcoming to people with different kinds of neurocognitive functioning, neurodivergence wouldn't be thought of as something that needs to be fixed.

Much of the medical world, unsurprisingly, disagrees. Many of these neurocognitive differences—traits and conditions that fall under the large umbrella of neurodivergence—are listed in the *Diagnostic and Statistical Manual of Mental Disorders* (DSM) as treatable diagnoses. A partial list of neurodivergent traits includes ADHD, autism, bipolar disorder, borderline personality disorder, Down syndrome, dyscalculia, dysgraphia, dyslexia, dyspraxia, intellectual disabilities, obsessive-compulsive disorder, sensory processing disorder (again, distinct from sensory processing sensitivity), social anxiety, and Tourette syndrome.

That's a lot to take in: so many different traits and conditions that affect people in different—visible and invisible—ways. Many of them frequently co-occur, and many have symptoms and presentations that are very similar and can be confused. There's a lot of misdiagnosis happening.

Interestingly, one trait that's conspicuously absent from most lists like this is sensory processing sensitivity (SPS) or high sensitivity. fMRI studies have shown "that SPS was associated with significantly greater activation in brain areas involved in higher order visual processing, which is more evidence for greater depth of processing in SPS compared to the general population."[4] Numerous researchers have found other differences between the brains of people with and without SPS,[5,6,7] and as we know from the sensitivityresearch.com site, about 30 percent of us are high on the sensitivity continuum, or have SPS.

In other words, our brains are different from the "typical," so we're neurodivergent.

What's in a name?

I know the term neurodivergent is controversial. Until there's more widespread awareness, understanding and acceptance of what it really means, there may be some stigma associated with it, just as there is with sensitivity. Some people prefer terms like *neuro-atypical* or *neurospicy,* although many in the neurodivergent community find the latter offensive to Black and Brown neurodivergent folks and trivializing in general. I've never been big on labels myself where people are concerned. I don't like being boxed in, and call it ego, but I don't think I can be described all that easily. A lot of labels simply aren't helpful, especially when they only cause division and create "otherness" (one reason some people don't like the word neurodivergent).

One of the many things I love about the neurodivergent community is the emphasis on using language the individual prefers. So I'm not suggesting that anyone adopt any particular term. When referring to yourself, use whatever you're comfortable with, and when referring to someone else, use the term *they* prefer.

ADHD

All that said, sometimes labels are useful: when they help us understand something that's not obvious. In my early 50s, I was diagnosed with ADHD (another term many in the neurodivergent community are unhappy with, for many reasons, but I'll use it here for lack of any broadly recognized alternative). You may know some late-diagnosed ADHDers—there are a lot of us around! It's easy to be skeptical; I'm still skeptical myself. Why have the numbers of adult women with ADHD skyrocketed in just the last few years?

There are a lot of reasonable theories. Studies have gotten more inclusive: Until fairly recently, most medical research focused on middle-class white males, and as it turns out, traits like ADHD and others can present very differently by gender. If healthcare providers are only equipped to identify specific behaviors in young white males, then anyone of any other age, race, or gender is less likely to be diagnosed, and any conditions that present differently from what they're used to seeing may not be recognized at all.[8]

There's also the fact that until fairly recently we weren't being bombarded by more information from more sources than ever before. When I was a kid, there were no laptops, no cell phones, no social media platforms. Imagine—or remember? No email or texting, no Facebook or Insta, no Slack or Discord, no Marco Polo, no Bluesky. We had fewer things that could distract us, fewer things to keep track of. Are the rising numbers of ADHD diagnoses just a result of electronic bombardment and data overload?

I don't have the answers; I still have my own questions. I decided to seek a diagnosis after several conversations with a colleague who shared her own ADHD journey at a conference where we both gave talks. Much of what she described resonated with me, despite big differences in age and life experience. And I had long struggled with focusing, with getting high-quality sleep, with impulsiveness, all closely associated with the trait. So I sought out a medical practice that specializes in working with patients with ADHD. After filling out an extremely long, detailed intake form, followed by an in-depth intake session with the provider, I was told I clearly met the diagnostic criteria for ADHD and given information about medication, which I decided to put aside for the time being.

I had conflicting feelings about the diagnosis. It made sense in some ways—that's why I'd gone for the assessment in the first place. There was also something that felt a little bit off, but I couldn't put my finger on it. Maybe it felt too easy or too quick, despite all the questions I'd answered. Maybe it was the sense that I hadn't fundamentally changed that much from when I was a kid—I'd always been different—so if it was so clear now, why had it never come up as a possibility then? (This, despite knowing about the differences in gender presentation and other issues mentioned earlier.)

At a second telehealth visit with the doctor, who assured me that medication would help with my ongoing challenges with focus and sleep, I decided to try it. Because I've always been sensitive to drugs of any kind and have had unexpected or unpleasant reactions, I wanted to start at a very low dose. At my four-week follow-up appointment, I told him that I wasn't noticing much of a difference; he suggested I increase the dosage slightly. But I had to switch providers because I'd started my own business, and the practice he belonged to was expensive and didn't accept my new insurance. I didn't want to make any other changes at the same time, and more medication would require more follow-up visits. I ended up going off the pills.

When I asked him for my records so I could give them to my new doctor, I read through all the notes from my three visits and found a bunch of inaccuracies: symptoms I hadn't listed (like losing things—I rarely do and wouldn't have said this) and results that were different from what I'd experienced (the notes said I'd felt improvement from the medication). There were enough discrepancies to make me question how closely he was paying attention—and the accuracy of the diagnosis. That's how the practice makes money, after all: by diagnosing ADHD and prescribing pills and follow-up visits. (I'm not suggesting they were unethical. I didn't get that sense. But at the very least, there was a lack of attention to detail that bothered me.)

I found a psychiatrist in my new insurance network whose profile said he worked with ADHD patients, and made an appointment. (Knowing about the potential gender differences in presentation, I looked for a female provider who could do the assessment; I couldn't find one in my network.) After another long intake form and a very short phone call, he told me I didn't meet the diagnostic criteria and was probably just stressed. And I was dismissed.

This doctor didn't inspire my confidence either. His questions were textbook, circa 1985: Did I have trouble sitting still? Had I caused trouble in school? Because I had been an excellent student and wasn't obviously hyperactive, he decided I couldn't possibly have ADHD.

Frustrated, I gave up on trying to get an accurate diagnosis. I assumed that I do have some ADHD traits and would have to figure out how to deal with it on my own.

Autism

Fast-forward a year and a half. While researching for this book and interviewing highly sensitive/high-sensory women leaders, I was introduced to Clare Kumar, speaker, executive performance coach, and host of the Happy Space Podcast (did you catch the HSP in there?). Between our first conversation and a much longer interview, I listened to several episodes of Clare's podcast—which turned my world upside-down.

A few months before we met, Clare had interviewed speaker, author, content marketing expert, and creativity coach Melanie Deziel. Melanie received an autism diagnosis in her 30s and is "on a mission to help one million undiagnosed women discover their autistic identity."[9] Her conversation with Melanie brought up so many memories and questions for her that Clare took a self-assessment after the interview and discovered that she's also autistic. She decided to pursue a more formal assessment with a healthcare provider—which she described to me as an "assessment-lite"—and her self-diagnosis was confirmed. (Within the autistic community, self-diagnosis is valid and accepted, for a number of reasons. Getting a medical diagnosis can be challenging: it can be very expensive. It can be difficult to find a provider who's neurodiversity-affirming, qualified to conduct the required assessments and up-to-date in their understanding of what autism can look like in different people. And if you do find such a person and have the money to pay, it can take months or longer to get your first appointment. Choosing to go this route is a decision not to be taken lightly.)

After listening to Clare's story and her interview with Melanie, I was fascinated. As had happened with my ADHDer colleague at the conference, there were several things both Clare and Melanie mentioned that sparked memories or connections for me. So I took the same online self-assessment.

Then I took about 11 more. And took a few more than once.

The results?

Inconclusive.

A couple of the tests, designed to measure things like "empathy quotient" (according to the test designer, a low score might indicate autism) and "systemizing quotient" (in this case, a high score might be an indicator), said that I wasn't autistic. I scored high on the former and low on the latter. (Note: The empathy assessment's accuracy and relevance has been called into question by a lot of people, experts included.)

On a few, my scores were positive, suggesting that I am. And on the rest, I came out in the "likely" or "probably" range, according to the test designers. Confusingly, a couple said that although I probably wasn't autistic, I showed some autistic traits. I'm still trying to understand what that means and the difference between being autistic and "having autistic traits." (Side note: I had to laugh at myself just reflecting on my own process. Taking the tests over and over again and quibbling with the way a lot of the questions were worded could both be taken as signs of autistic traits, which was confirmed by several members of an autistic community on Facebook that I joined and asked about my experience.)

After taking the assessments and spending many, many hours online researching, I came across some YouTubers whose videos—accounts of their own late diagnoses and how their lives had changed—brought me to tears. I found several by female psychologists and psychotherapists who had identified as HSPs for years and had just, in the past year or two, learned that they were autistic too. I read and watched personal stories of adult women who had always felt misunderstood, different, until they learned—some, like me, in their 50s or later—that they were autistic. And that autism often doesn't look the way we thought it did.

AuDHD

A lot of these women identify as AuDHDers, meaning that, like me, they have the frequently co-occurring (and, confusingly, often conflicting) traits of ADHD and autism together. I'm seeing and hearing this more and more, and learning about it and hearing their stories is what finally made my earlier ADHD diagnosis make more sense. The two things inform and temper each other.

ADHD trait: I've moved house a ridiculous number of times. I don't *enjoy* moving, but there's always been a good reason and I've done what I had to do.

Autistic trait: I'm a nester, and I hate the before-and-after chaos of moving; I can't think straight when surrounded by boxes and when I can't get to my things. So I pack as close to the move date as possible, and unpack immediately, even when I'm exhausted. I'm like an unpacking tornado. Friends and family joke about how every new place I move into looks like I've been there for years on day two.

Autistic trait: I have a lot of knick-knacks—crystals, artwork, pottery, things I've collected around the world—and I arrange them carefully on shelves and furniture throughout my home. It really bugs me when house cleaners move things (to clean!) and don't move them back where they belong.

ADHD trait: My desk often looks like a hurricane blew by, with sticky note pads and multiple notebooks in use and papers and stuff everywhere. And no one to blame but me.

Autistic trait: I become fascinated by things ("special interests") and spend hours going down rabbit holes to learn as much as I possibly can about them. This can be a topic or a hobby; with the hobbies, I might invest money, time, and energy and be passionate about them…

ADHD trait: …for a while. Then I get bored with that thing and move on to something else equally fascinating. (There are interests and passions I've had my entire life, like languages and crafts. But within those, my attention moves around a lot. I study one language or play with one kind of craft for a while and then try another.)

I love this LinkedIn post, shared by permission from neuroinclusion coach, consultant, and advocate Jodie Yorg:

> *My Autism:* Creating a thematic content calendar for LinkedIn will keep me on track and make posting consistent (she's very Hermione Granger).
>
> *My ADHD:* Wait. What? You want me to post about the same subject every Monday? BORING (she's very Ron Weasley).
>
> *My AuDHD:* I'll just put an X on the days I've written posts and write ideas on whatever Post-It I can find (she's very me).
>
> *Living my best life somewhere between totally all over it and flying by the seat of my pants.*

I know exactly how she feels.

I wrote earlier that sometimes labels can be helpful in understanding what isn't visible or obvious. In my case, neither the ADHD nor the autism label alone felt right or described me; when I learned about AuDHD, though, and read, watched and heard accounts from so many other late-diagnosed women, I felt like I'd found my home.

Can you be both an HSP and autistic?

The answer to this question depends on who you ask. At the time of this writing, there are three camps: those who believe they're essentially the same thing (many in the neurodivergent community consider "HSP" an ableist term for autism), those who believe they're different and you can be both, and those who believe they're mutually exclusive.

Many researchers are in the latter group. Bianca Acevedo, Elaine Aron, et al., published an article in 2018 called, "The functional highly sensitive brain: a review of the brain circuits underlying sensory processing sensitivity and seemingly related disorders."[10] They conclude that SPS engages different parts of the brain than autism, schizophrenia, and PTSD in certain functions, including "reward processing, memory, physiological homeostasis, self-other processing, empathy and awareness," so SPS is a distinct trait. In the Methods section of the article, though, the authors state that their review excluded studies of "milder forms" of autism, referring to "high-functioning autism" specifically (language that many in the autistic community don't favor, by the way), "to make for a strong comparison with SPS, as studies have tended to find differing results for samples low on Autism or with experimental paradigms that were not truly measuring empathy." They're essentially saying that if they were to include research with a broader definition or understanding of autism, it would be more difficult to show a difference between autism and SPS. I reached out to Acevedo to learn more. I wondered whether she'd done any more work in this area in the last six years or come across any differing information, given how much has changed in the understanding of autism in that time, but she was unavailable to talk with me.

I had a long and engaging conversation with Esther Bergsma, the author of *The Brain of the Highly Sensitive Person*, who enjoyed seeing my copy of her book with dozens of sticky flags marking passages I wanted to refer back to. After we talked, Esther followed up with a wealth of research on various aspects of high sensitivity. When I asked her the HSP/autistic question, she was in the third camp based on her knowledge of existing research. She listed the three main differences that have been shown between highly sensitive people and autistic people:

- Cognitive (as opposed to affective) empathy—the ability to truly understand someone else's emotional or mental state
- The ability to see both the big picture and the details
- The predictive brain—the unconscious process by which the brain uses prior knowledge to anticipate future events

Further into the conversation, Esther acknowledged there are a lot of questions that haven't yet been answered and probably won't be soon. We've emailed back and forth a few times since we spoke, and she's been very open to watching videos I've sent her way and considering the possibilities. We've each raised a few factors that likely contribute to the confusion: For one thing, concern about the accuracy of some diagnoses, which, given my own experiences, doesn't surprise me. Then there are likely unconscious (or even conscious) biases underlying some of the studies. Researchers often start with a hypothesis they're trying to either prove or disprove. And a lot of decisions are made in the course of the research that might be shaped by other existing research and contextual cues.

I have all three of the traits Esther listed above—cognitive empathy, the ability to see both the big picture and the details, and a predictive brain—and I know other late-diagnosed AuDHD women whom I strongly suspect also have all three. But there are so many factors to untangle. Autistic brains, for example, are known to be strong in pattern recognition. Are we just using pattern recognition skills in a different way? Having observed other people all our lives, do we get to the point where it becomes easier to see the patterns in emotions? Or to predict the future based on everything we've learned from the past?

Psychotherapist Julie Bjelland seems to believe you can be both an HSP and autistic. Julie's work has broadened from focusing on high sensitivity to encompassing adult-discovered autism since her own late diagnosis. Her website, a great resource for anyone just starting out on this journey, used to offer both a sensitivity quiz and an autism quiz, but as of this writing, they've been combined into one. A note above it says, "Historically, diagnostic criteria have overlooked how autism presents in women, contributing to an estimated 80 percent of autistic women remaining undiagnosed. I believe that many of the most sensitive women may be autistic without realizing it! Autism is a spectrum, meaning each individual experiences it uniquely."[11]

Clare Kumar also believes it's possible to be both: "It's such a great question. I've been wrestling with it; I think that sensory sensitivity is at play in multiple ways of being. For me, it makes sense. I know intimately well the traits of the highly sensitive person, and I feel that that definitely applies. When I look at the traits in autism that I identify with very strongly, there's a lot of overlap there, especially in the sensory piece in emotional regulation, emotional responsiveness, those things. I think where I see a difference is with autism, there's a clinging to logic and speaking up for social justice. And I don't see that commonly in highly sensitive people."

I disagree with Clare on just the last part. The logic piece is true for me and others I know, but it's not a topic I tend to raise in conversations about sensitivity and autism; I don't feel as strongly about it as I do about some of the other traits. The social justice piece of her statement surprised me, though, as social justice issues come up frequently with my coaching clients, mastermind members, and colleagues who identify as HSPs.

A lingering question for me is whether these are all distinct traits or conditions—SPS, autism and ADHD, for example—or simply (more) evidence that we're all wired a little bit differently. Remember my mixing board metaphor? What if every trait associated with all these conditions were individual channels on the board? Sensitivity to sound, to taste, to smell. Pattern recognition. Impulsivity. Cognitive empathy. Logic. Predictive thinking. Seeing the big picture. Attention to details. Deep sense of social justice. Add in all the traits associated with dyslexia and dyscalculia and Tourette syndrome and the numerous other "disorders" that make us who we are. Each adjustment on the mixing board has a slightly different effect on the sound being played.

Maybe *I'm* getting too woo-woo now, but another image I have is of a giant, cosmic buffet table, full of dishes of different kinds. Appetizers, entrees, salads, and desserts. Some finger food, some dishes that require cutlery and a little more finesse. Each food is one of the traits above. At some point before we're born, our souls walk down the buffet line with huge plates, picking and choosing the traits we'll go through this lifetime with—the gifts and the challenges. Insert your own spiritual beliefs here.

Back to earth—and labels—for a moment: Discovering that AuDHD might be why I've always struggled with certain things has been life-changing. I've not only learned more about myself, I've found a welcoming community of people who struggle with similar things or in similar ways. I've also learned to laugh at myself in a way I never could before. The ADHD vs. autistic trait conflicts are pretty funny with a little perspective, and it's validating to know that other smart, talented, high-achieving women have similar challenges all the time. None of us is broken, or crazy, or alone.

Takeaways

- ☑ Neurodiversity is simply acknowledgment of the naturally occurring differences in all our brains. Groups or organizations of two or more are neurodiverse; individuals are neurodivergent, as distinguished from neurotypical, which might be more of a philosophical construct than a physiological reality.
- ☑ The neurodiversity paradigm states that differences in neurocognitive function are normal and not deficits or disorders.
- ☑ There's a fair amount of overlap in "symptoms" and traits between high sensitivity and other types of neurodivergence such as ADHD, autism, AuDHD, and other conditions.
- ☑ The labels are less important than self-awareness, empathy, and compassion for—and acceptance of—ourselves and others, and learning to ask for what we need.

3

Empathy and its darker side

Highly perceptive people come in all shapes, sizes, and genders, and from all backgrounds. As different as we are, our shared trait of high sensitivity typically comes with predictable strengths—I call them superpowers—and challenges that often accompany them. One of the most common strengths is deep empathy, which can show up at an early age.

I asked Kristina Foge, a customer success leader, how her high sensitivity showed up when she was a child. "I was a straight-A student; my report cards were amazing. I was the model kid. I loved school because I was good at it. I was adored because of the straight A's, the little lace socks that my mother made me wear, and the cute little shoes and dresses," Kristina remembered.

"My brother, on the other hand, had an attention problem. He would make noise in church. He was kind of a rabble rouser. He was the kid who got negative attention because it worked, so he used it. Every Sunday, my (step-)grandmother asked me where

I wanted to go to lunch. She never asked my brother. And I got tired of it. And I finally just looked at my little brother and asked, 'Where would *you* like to go?' He said, 'How about Burger King?' It was one of his favorite places. *I* didn't like Burger King. But I looked at my grandmother and said, 'I would like to go to Burger King.'

"I didn't say that my brother wanted to go. Because I just knew that wouldn't work with her. Even as a child, I was paying attention to other people. My empathy button was active when I was six or seven. That's why I was brave enough to fix the problem. Now, I wasn't brave enough to look at my grandmother and tell her she was being mean, because she was an adult. But that's what she was doing. My little brother—I could see his hurt in the fact that he was never asked. It was never, 'Hey, this week we'll go where one of you wants to go, and next week the other one gets to choose.' She never did that. So I had to fix it."

It would be remarkable for most kids of six or seven to be so attuned to the feelings and expectations of others. But deep empathy isn't unusual at all for highly perceptive children. Minette Norman, award-winning author and international speaker on inclusive leadership and psychological safety, remembers watching the movie *Born Free* at six years old, and sobbing when they let Elsa, the lioness, go.

"The other thing that I was very sensitive about as a really little kid, which a lot of little kids aren't," Minette told me, "is that I was always very worried about, and caring about, old people. I was always asking, 'Are they okay, do we need to do something?' That was important to who I am and who I was, who I've always been."

Empathy is a topic that comes up in almost every conversation I have with highly perceptive people, and, in this context, it's always acknowledged as a gift. Clearly, being able to truly understand someone else's feelings, perspectives, and experiences is helpful in all kinds of situations and relationships, personal and professional. We'll talk more about empathy in the chapters on HSPs in the workplace and highly perceptive leadership.

As with many innate strengths, though, being deeply empathetic can come with its own challenges. I talked a little in Chapter 1 about empaths who carry around other people's emotions and physical pain. When you feel too much—whether as a result of taking on other people's feelings or simply being empathetic and emotional in general—one not-uncommon response is to use alcohol or drugs to shut the feelings out. Another is to build walls in self-defense, which not only keep others' energy and emotions out—they also serve really well to hide behind. It's hard for people to get to know (or bully or insult or reject) the real you when you're behind the walls of a fortress.

More than one highly perceptive leader told me that colleagues think of them as efficient, highly competent, no-nonsense. Sometimes even curt or abrupt. Definitely *not* warm and fuzzy. And yet, when they felt safe enough with me to let their defenses down, it was so easy to see how much they felt and cared.

Looking back at several jobs I had in my 20s, 30s, and even 40s, I'm sure some people I worked with would say something similar about me. Victoria Bullis's bubble may have helped me repel unwanted company on public transit, but it took me a lot longer to learn how to create healthy boundaries so that I could be open, be myself, and still protect myself from outside influences or harsh or toxic environments.

I built a lot of walls. I'm still learning how to knock some of them down.

People-pleasing and the struggle to say no

A different kind of challenge for those who are deeply empathetic—who perceive others' emotions so easily and clearly—is the need to make other people happy, to be liked, to avoid being judged negatively. Amy Ballantyne, executive coach and host of the podcast *Power To The People Pleasers,* regularly interviews people who, at some point in their lives, said yes or did things to please others, or at least to avoid displeasing them.

I asked Amy the question she asks her guests at the start of every episode: Has she ever been a people pleaser, and if so, how did it show up in her life?

"I call myself a recovering people pleaser because it still does rear its ugly head now and then," she responded, "but I've seen it come up in my life in many, many ways over the years."

Amy shared a recent example that tested her resolve to stop people-pleasing. For years, she served as the team manager for her son's "rep" hockey team, managing a large budget, handling all the hotel bookings for 18 families for multiple tournaments, taking care of all the team's paperwork and accounting—on top of her own business and family commitments. And she was good at it.

Every year, the new coach asked her if she'd like to continue. "I would just say yes, because, *and these are the words to listen for,* because I'm good at it, and because it'll be fine, it'll be easy, I already know what to do. All the things that we say when we're just trying to convince ourselves that it's a good idea. And I did that year after year after year, and this year, a bunch of things were happening in our life at the time."

She was preparing for her second TEDx talk and several other speaking engagements as well as serving a huge client load. Her family was moving to a new home, too. She had a lot on her plate. "So I made the decision to say no this time, but it was very uncomfortable. *Very* uncomfortable and very difficult. And, of course, the coach knew that I could do this job easily and effectively. When I said no, they pushed back and asked if I was sure. Not to pressure me, but because they knew I could do it. I said no again, but I still felt, in that moment, *I don't want to let people down.*"

But Amy checked in with herself and held onto her truth: The opportunity was no longer aligned with her goals, so she said no. And that no not only gave her space to focus on her priorities—it also gave other people the chance to get involved and learn how to manage the behind-the-scenes realities of a rep hockey team.

Given the societal expectations so many of us grew up with, it's tempting to assume that people-pleasing is a "female trait." Not so, though: Amy's had plenty of clients and podcast guests who identify as male and have struggled with this all their lives. From my own personal and professional observations, I'd agree that it's a challenge many highly perceptive people face, regardless of gender.

People-pleasing shows up in a lot of different ways. We might offer to do something we don't particularly want to do or go along with a plan that we're not 100 percent behind, to fit in or avoid rejection. We might say yes when we'd really rather say no because it's easier than risking someone else's disappointment, anger, or worse. We might even be programmed by our families or cultures to feel that it's selfish to do what we want and should always take care of others first.

However it shows up, the only way to put an end to people-pleasing is to decide how you want to show up in the world and what conditions you need to become that version of you. Another way of saying this? Boundaries.

Boundaries aren't just to keep people out

"Boundaries" is a buzzword these days, which makes it easy to dismiss. But there's a reason boundaries are coming up in so many books and podcasts and articles: They define our territory—where we begin and other people end.

Boundaries also separate acceptable from unacceptable behavior. And each of us gets to decide what's acceptable and unacceptable to and for us.

Making these decisions is critical for our mental, emotional, and physical health.

For all the talk about boundaries, it's shocking how many of us don't bother to set them. Or we might have some, but we never communicate them to other people or even honor them ourselves. And without communicating, honoring, and enforcing our boundaries, we might as well not have any at all.

Common areas that need boundaries:

- When you work—including days and times when you'll check and respond to emails, texts, or chats, and answer phone calls

- How much down time or alone time you need—and how much time you want to spend with partners, friends, and family
- When and how much you sleep—according to how much you need, not how much time is left over after you've taken care of everyone else
- Physical space—creating privacy, separating work from "life" if that's helpful or important to you, designing spaces that meet your needs and support you
- Wellness—exercise, diet, spiritual practice, and anything else you need to function at your best
- Finances—whether you share them with another or manage your own, it's important to know your resources and limits
- Communication—if conversations about certain topics or with certain people set you off or end badly every time, be clear about what's off-limits and with whom

And these are just a start.

If you want to establish some boundaries in your life and aren't sure where to begin, start with the topics listed above and reflect on any patterns that come up for you.

Where are the pain points?

Which areas cause the most stress? Which are bringing up the most resistance right now? These are good indicators that you already know where you need boundaries the most.

What gets left behind?

What are the things that are constantly getting rescheduled or simply left undone? Often, these are the most personal—health-related activities, like regular exercise or medical appointments, or activities that bring us joy, like creative pursuits or things we do just for fun. I've heard from too many perceptive women in particular that they feel guilty taking time for themselves, especially—but not exclusively—if they have kids.

What do you want your life to look like?

An exercise I frequently do with clients is ask them to choose a time in the not-too-distant future when they're happy or content, when things are going well in all aspects of their life. Not too far away, maybe between six months and three years from now. I ask them to imagine themselves in their life at that time and offer a series of prompts; then I give them a few moments in silence to notice and absorb. When I gently bring them back and ask about the experience, in many cases, this simple visioning exercise highlights some important changes they want to start making now to create this future reality. I explain how to guide yourself through this exercise in the book's Conclusion.

Communicating your boundaries

Now that you've identified where in your life you need new boundaries, it's time to let anyone who might be affected by them know. As Amy Ballantyne pointed out when her husband assumed she'd help with his volunteer project, as she'd always done before, "This is no longer who I want to be, having people make the assumption that I will just say yes to whatever they're asking me to do. Everyone deserves to be asked, and to be given the chance to evaluate whether or not a commitment fits into their schedule. In my husband's defense, I had been the people pleaser for our entire time together, so why wouldn't he just assume that I would drop everything to help with his volunteer project? Just because it's in my heart and mind that I'm making this transition in my life doesn't mean that the other person knows what I'm thinking. It's my opportunity to inform, share, and communicate my new boundaries."

Some people will be more understanding than others, and some communication will be trickier. There are plenty of books and resources out there on how to have these difficult conversations, so I won't go into more detail here. Three points I continually remind myself and my clients of when boundary conversations come up:

o **Clarity is kindness.** Being clear in your own mind about why you're doing what you're doing will help you share your reasoning with others (if appropriate).

o **Very little is either urgent or permanent.** Before you respond to a request that crosses a boundary, pause, take a breath, and, if you need it, ask for more time. If you change your mind later—or your availability changes—you're allowed to change your response.

o **The best response isn't always yes or no.** Sometimes it's possible to negotiate and find an outcome that satisfies everyone.

For some boundaries, like your working hours, you don't necessarily have to proactively tell people, at least right away—and unless you're making a big change.

If your work hours have always "officially" ended around 5 p.m., for example, but you always work later, where's the boundary breakdown happening? Is someone else regularly asking you to work late? Are you working late because you've spent most of your day helping others, or in meetings? Or are you doing it because there's so much to do or you're trying to get ahead of it all?

Your responses to these questions will determine your next steps. If someone else keeps asking you to work late, then a conversation has to happen. You can support that conversation (and the boundary) by making sure that your work calendar settings accurately reflect your availability and you're blocking out your personal time. If the reason you're working late every night is *you*, though, it's not about communication—it's about honoring your own decisions and boundaries.

Honoring our own boundaries

While I was writing *Perceptive*, Heather Thompson, career coach and host of the podcast *Recipes for Success*, invited me on her show to talk about boundaries as part of a series on the habits of highly successful women.[1] Heather commented that some of the things I described in our conversation sound like habits. And they are, in a way: Habits are the behaviors I've adopted to support the boundaries I've set for myself.

When you're getting in your own way, it can help to consider your habits. What behaviors are you so used to that you just do them naturally, whether they're good for you or not?

I need at least eight or nine hours of good sleep to feel and function at my best. A light sleeper with a lot of sensitivities, I know, from many years of experience, that several things will prevent me from getting that sleep: being on my computer or phone; watching TV late at night; drinking caffeine at any time of day; and drinking alcohol or eating anything within several hours of going to bed are a few of these. So I have boundaries around each of them for my own benefit, and I've changed my habits to support those boundaries.

To honor them, I eat dinner early. I don't drink caffeine and rarely drink alcohol—and if I do, I'm careful about how much and how late I drink and about having a lot of water with or after it. I have the Do Not Disturb function on my phone set automatically, so at a certain time I just put it down and forget about it for the night.

I *try* to get off my computer at a reasonable time. I also have a bad habit of telling myself I'm just going to finish one last thing and then noticing that it's an hour or two or three later and I'm stiff and thirsty and it's past time to have stopped working for the evening. If this sounds familiar, give yourself some grace—and remind yourself why you decided to set that boundary in the first place. Then keep working on the habit you want to establish.

Why bother?

I can't tell you why you need boundaries in your life; I can only tell you why I need them in mine. It's about protecting my emotional, mental, and physical health so I can be the best version of me. That, in turn, impacts my work and everyone around me.

When I'm coaching a client, I start with the premise that they have the answers they need within them; it's my job to ask questions that'll help them discover those answers. So the questions I'll leave you with around boundaries are:

- What isn't working in your life right now?
- What change(s) could you make so it would go more smoothly?

Struggling with things like boundaries can actually give us more empathy for others. While we may all have areas in our lives where we're better at maintaining boundaries, having a few we're not as strong in seems to be universal.

Takeaways

☑ Empathy is a gift that highly perceptive people tend to have in abundance, and it can show up at an early age.

☑ Being so attuned to others, though, has its challenges. It's not uncommon for HSPs, empaths, and others with this gift to build walls or develop other defense mechanisms to stop feeling so much.

☑ People-pleasing can be a way of trying to prevent bad things from happening or to fit in and avoid feeling excluded. But it's not usually in our own best interest.

☑ Setting boundaries helps ensure that we make decisions and take actions that align with our values and goals, and generally keeps us healthy and functioning well.

☑ Communicating our boundaries to those affected by them doesn't have to be hard, and is both necessary and kind.

☑ Sometimes the one who struggles the most with our boundaries is . . . us. Reflecting on why we put them in place can remind us why honoring them is important. How do we want to show up in the world, and what will support us in becoming that person?

Connecting the dots

Krystal Jones, another customer success leader I spoke with, describes the way her mind works as Sherlock Holmes-like. She's a problem solver, easily making quick connections among lots of pieces of information.

She can see several steps ahead, a strength valuable not only for solving immediate problems but also for strategic planning.

This highly perceptive, self-described people person has plenty of other gifts, too, including the ability to read a room and understand what a team needs and how to connect with, energize, and motivate people: "Getting people who wouldn't normally be talking, talking; picking up on the shift in someone's behavior. And then sensing gestures, facial expressions; I'm seeing all of it."

You'd think every organization wants a leader like this, right?

Except… She's been passed over twice for promotions she believes she's earned and left out of key meetings. The lack of transparency around these things is hard for her because she's so perceptive. She picks up on signs that other people don't and knows when she's not being told the truth.

After learning about high sensory perception and identifying strongly with certain aspects of the trait, Krystal had more insight into this challenge: "Because I see things and I'm a couple steps ahead, I'm trying to be helpful, so I'm interjecting and trying to be the problem solver. I think some people think, 'oh, she thinks she knows it all.'"

I can identify with this so easily—and painfully. I've heard different versions of it from other highly perceptive leaders and experienced it myself in more than one corporate role.

I used to dread getting feedback during performance reviews. I always put my heart and soul into my work, and yet I frequently felt misunderstood. More than once, I was told by my boss that I was seen as negative or focused on challenges or obstacles, rather than encouraging possibilities. That I was cutting down other people's ideas.

As someone who deeply values both inclusion and creativity, that was heartbreaking to hear. It was the exact opposite of what I wanted and intended, and it hurt that my colleagues had that perception of me.

Learning that my brain processes information differently—research has shown that highly sensitive brains light up in different places at different times than in "neurotypical" brains—was life-changing.

Esther Bergsma, in *The Brain of the Highly Sensitive Person*, writes,

> Studies into the functioning of the highly sensitive brain show that HSPs are strongly focused on the social group. I have called this the optimal-option-ambition: the action that best serves the group is preferred. HSPs are strongly

focused on the interests of the group and often subordinate their own interests.[1]

A few paragraphs later, after describing the way HSPs perceive, process, and react to stimuli, she notes, "the advantage of this way of processing information" is that "it leads to more effective action. The energy it takes to better notice and more deeply process all stimuli thus yields added value in effectiveness."[2]

I realized that not everyone was seeing several steps ahead, as I was. Some were simply brainstorming, trying to come up with as many ideas as possible, regardless of feasibility. My natural tendency to problem-solve—combined with my desire to help the team achieve success—meant that I was always (although not entirely consciously) processing all the connections among data points, following the logical progression of the idea or plan, and seeing why something wouldn't work, and therefore why we should leave it behind and move on to another idea. I was trying to help the team be more efficient and effective.

Which makes me, by the way, awful at playing by the usual rules of brainstorming—in which critiquing ideas isn't allowed in the early stages.

Understanding all this now doesn't change the way my brain works, but it means that I can consciously choose to respond and communicate differently when I'm in situations like this from now on. I can wait to say anything until we reach the sorting and filtering stage of the process. Or "Yes, and" the ideas by celebrating the nuggets that have promise and suggesting changes or additions that might nudge the original suggestion in a more effective direction.

Learning all of this was validating on a very personal level. There wasn't anything wrong with me; I wasn't a mean person or a bad team player. I genuinely was trying to be helpful and could now give myself some grace and understanding for the negative peer feedback.

It was also a helpful reminder that just as other people didn't understand how my brain worked, which resulted in my intentions being misunderstood, it was very possible that I was misunderstanding others' intentions, too. Something to be aware of and look out for.

Strategic thinking: Seeing both the big picture and the details

As I mentioned, this ability to see several steps ahead is a common strength highly perceptive leaders share—as well as a common source of frustration. I don't share stories from male-identifying HSP leaders in this book because I work mostly with women. Over the course of many conversations with highly perceptive people of all genders, what struck me is that while the trait itself is gender-agnostic, the way it affects us depends on a number of factors, including social and cultural norms.

An example of a difference I've noticed: When I've spoken with highly perceptive male leaders, the single biggest frustration they've all mentioned around having this quality at work is having to go along with executive decisions they disagreed with—having to communicate them to their teams and support plans that they could see wouldn't work and knew were wrong. In a few cases, this has been a deciding factor for these leaders in leaving the corporate world and starting their own business. In others, it's been a prompt to find another role and/or another organization that would value their input, clear vision, and strength in strategic thinking and planning. If I bring this up with female leaders, they agree that it's a problem, but it's not typically their biggest challenge or one they raise on their own.

Back to the ability to process large amounts of information and make connections quickly: Another gift that I suspect is related is the ability to see both the big picture and the details at the same time. Most people tend to see either the forest or the trees—but not both. All the highly perceptive people I've spoken with strongly relate to this—for better and worse, as with other aspects of our high sensory perception.

For better: We can see the whole plan or system laid out and understand all the individual steps or parts. This is ideal for managing large programs, initiatives, or teams; you need to know how all the pieces or people come together to support the whole.

It was also helpful for me in my career as an editor: The details—the word usage and syntax, the grammar and punctuation, the flow of the copy—were critical, and I also had to understand the larger structure of the work and ensure that all the sections flowed together.

For worse: Many of the HSPs I know call themselves "recovering perfectionists" (myself included). When you notice all the tiny details and see how they fit together, it's hard not to want them all to be perfect. We tend to have extremely high standards and expectations for ourselves and others, and no detail is too small for our attention.

This creates two problems. First, we can get far too wrapped up in details that aren't that important in the overall scheme of things and spend precious time and energy trying to get them exactly right. I know I'm guilty of that; I'll sit down to make a small change to my website and end up fiddling with fonts and word spacing for ages. Yes, it's important that the site looks clean and professional. Will every visitor notice that I used an [H2] tag instead of an [H3] or that a caption isn't exactly centered down to the pixel? And even if they do, will they judge my services because of it? Probably not.

Second, knowing we can take care of the details and handle them well can prevent us from delegating, which is another way to ensure that we're not spending our time and energy efficiently or effectively.

Minette Norman, the author and speaker we met in Chapter 3, started her career as a technical writer. When she was first promoted, she struggled with delegating and perfectionism.

"I think this was really part of my professional growth," Minette shared with me. "It was when I went from being an individual contributor, a writer, to managing a team of writers. That's where it really showed up for me because I could do all of their jobs and felt I could do them better. It's so hard to pull back and not be in the minutiae, and honestly, that was a process for me to get through. I felt I needed to attend *all* the meetings, read *all* the drafts. And gradually what cures you of that is when you start to manage people who do things you can't do.

"So when I moved from managing writers to managing engineers, I couldn't be in the details because I didn't even *understand* all the details. That, I think, is what cured me of that need. But when I was managing the work that I could do myself, it was really hard."

It's a challenge. I faced it myself when I first started managing writers and content teams. What finally cured me of the habit was realizing that there simply wasn't enough time in the day or week to do everything I was responsible for—never mind do the work of people on my team too. And if that weren't enough, I eventually figured out what a huge disservice I was doing them by not giving them the opportunity to learn, uplevel their skills, and prove themselves.

Intuition and trust

A few years after the burnout I wrote about in the Introduction, I moved back to the United States. I'd spent more than three years living in three different countries and cultures in South America and Europe, immersing myself in languages, art, and other things I enjoyed. And taking the time I needed to heal.

I was finally ready to start working full-time again, and excited about the opportunity to do something different. I applied for jobs in operations management. Although not entirely new—I'd served as COO for a startup English language institute in Ecuador and managed operations at a national nonprofit, where I oversaw admin, IT, and HR in addition to my main role as communications director—it was a very different field from content, editorial, and communications, where I'd spent most of my career. My résumé didn't shout operations.

I got interviews for interesting roles but never made it past the first stage. Looking back, I see clearly why I had so much trouble: I didn't *really* want any of those jobs, and the interviewers could probably tell.

I needed to get back to work and didn't want to do what I'd been doing for decades, but didn't have the experience recruiters were looking for for jobs that sounded interesting. A conundrum. Then an opportunity came up, more or less out of the blue: A three-week fellowship and study program in intercultural communications hosted on a scenic college campus in Portland, Oregon, not far from where I was living.

In short order, I applied, was accepted, packed my bags, and spent the first part of the summer with an incredible group of instructors and learners from all over the world.

The courses were challenging and exciting, and I loved the program. It reminded me of a dream I'd had as a child: For a while, when asked what I wanted to do when I grew up, I'd say I wanted to find a company that would sponsor me to live in every country in the world so I could learn every language and help the world communicate better.

A program in intercultural communication couldn't have been more perfect. I only wished I'd known earlier that such a thing existed.

Returning home after the program, I started researching. What could I do that would involve my passion for languages and cultures, my background in communications, my extensive experience traveling and living abroad? I found an answer: a master's program in international education management. I was already familiar with the school that offered it—I'd been accepted into their master's program in translation and interpretation my senior year in college and decided, in the end, not to go.

I'd always regretted that, and then it was too late, since I'd been away from the languages for so long. Here was a chance for a sort of do-over, and it wouldn't require the language fluency that professional translation does. It sounded like another perfect fit.

Except for one tiny detail. The small private graduate school was quite expensive, and I didn't qualify for any grants or major scholarships. I'd have had to take out a very large loan and start over in my early 50s in a field that wasn't known for paying well. It was a scary thought.

I applied and was accepted into the master's program. At the same time, I was invited to interview for a job I'd already forgotten I'd applied for: an editorial manager position based in Switzerland—in the international education division of a huge company with offices all over the world.

I told the VP I interviewed with that I was considering the master's program and had to make a decision soon; they accelerated the process for me. To my surprise, since they had candidates already based in Europe who wouldn't require visa sponsorship, they offered me the job.

School or job? I made lists of pros and cons for each. I talked with friends and family members. I did visioning exercises. I agonized over the decision.

I was excited about the graduate program. I loved the location in Monterey, California; I'd lived there briefly years earlier. I really wanted to study and to learn, and the curriculum sounded interesting and useful.

But I kept coming back to the enormous debt I'd graduate with, and how challenging it might be to get a job in the field with a salary that would allow me to pay it off.

I finally made the decision out of fear, not out of love or excitement. I took the job I didn't want to do anymore, in a country that I knew already wouldn't be a great cultural fit for me. (Side note: This was based on my intercultural studies and Hofstede's cultural dimensions theory—not random bias. Hofstede's work had helped me understand why some of the cultures I'd spent time in felt much more comfortable to me than others.)

I went with my head and not my heart.

The salary was decent by Swiss standards. They upgraded my title to editorial director without me asking, because I'd been a director in previous roles. And I knew the company was open to people changing positions and locations when they'd been there a while; I told myself I could stay in that role for a year and then move into another division and role within the company in another part of the world.

I ignored the little red flags I noticed along the way. Like the fact that I'd never seen the VP, my new boss, even though we'd had many conversations and weeks of emails back and forth; there was always some reason she couldn't be on video.

I'd asked to interview in person in Lucerne, to meet her and her leadership team, see the office space and get a feel for the location. I would be hiring a new team and wanted to know what I was going into so I could be clear and honest with them. My request was declined.

There were other things that bothered me, too, but nothing I could do about any of them. I never questioned, for example, why they'd chosen me over a European candidate for whom the hiring process would've been quicker and less complicated. And all the friends and family I spoke with thought I'd be nuts to choose the master's program over what sounded, on paper, like a good job in a country they all wanted to visit.

So, decision made, I declined the grad school offer (again) and waited for my Swiss visa to come through. And waited, and waited. It took months longer than I'd been told to expect, and as I wasn't yet getting paid and had no idea how much longer it would take, it was a stressful time. I couldn't book flights or make any arrangements. The company kept sending me revised contracts with new start dates, and I waited.

Eventually, the visa was approved, and I packed to move halfway around the world, again. As soon as I landed and settled into temporary accommodations, I started looking for an apartment to rent. I dealt with all the paperwork required by the Swiss bureaucracy and learned how to buy groceries in Swiss German. I knew how to do all the things you need to do when moving to a new country, so I did them, almost on autopilot.

It took less than two weeks for me to admit to myself that I'd made a huge mistake.

My boss in person was very different from the empathetic executive I'd talked and emailed with so many times from thousands of miles away. The job was laughably different from what I'd been led to expect. The team culture, under my VP, was toxic, and the company overall not much better (it was also very odd). And I'd been correct in my assumption that Swiss culture wasn't a great fit for me, either.

I tried hard to make it work, despite coming home after work crying from frustration night after night. My rental contract had a four-month-notice clause—as did my employment contract. I'd been there about two months when I finally gave up trying and resigned. The furniture and belongings I'd shipped from the US hadn't even arrived yet.

How had everything gone so extremely wrong?

Like most highly perceptive people I've talked with and read about, I've gotten strong intuitive hits all my life. I know things without knowing *how* I know them. I haven't found research that specifically explores a connection between HSPs and intuition, but to me it makes sense: Our brains are always actively making connections and processing data.

In an article in *Psychology Today* on the biological basis of intuition, author Thomas Verny, MD, writes,

> Intuition relies on evolutionarily older, automatic, unconscious, and fast mental processing, primarily to save our brains time or energy. . . . Intuition later in life arises from the accumulation of knowledge and experiences that are processed and stored in our brain's neural networks, as well as other cells and tissues in our bodies, allowing us to access this information quickly, often unconsciously.[3]

It's logical that HSPs, who are continually downloading and processing more data than others, have tons of information to access intuitively.

As Verny explains, the gut and the heart are connected to the brain and both contain neural tissue. So when we get a "gut feeling" or "know something in our heart," the information we're accessing is all coming from the same source.

My story is full of examples of challenges highly perceptive people can face: Our high standards and expectations compel us to put 150 percent of ourselves into everything we do, which frequently leads to burnout. We're most invested when we care deeply about the cause or subject matter; it can be harder to put energy into things we don't care about, but we do it anyway because of our strong sense of conscientiousness and responsibility.

We often have the answers we need already, but we've been taught not to trust them. Because we see both the big picture and all the details, we are prone to overthinking—as Krystal Jones told me, she tends to "perseverate, to ruminate." We want everything to be right, to work out perfectly. We ask our friends and family members and colleagues, hoping that someone else will validate our own inexplicable knowing, and when that doesn't happen, we can get stuck in an endless cycle of questioning ourselves and rewriting lists of pros and cons.

And when we have to make a final decision, we often make the one we "should" make, that our head tells us to make—the one that comes from fear.

Dr. Verny concludes in the article,

> There is growing evidence suggesting that all humans are born with a basic ability for intuitive thinking and that, as we mature, as our links between the embodied mind, emotional processing, and intuitive thinking strengthen with experience, we may get better at it. *Of course, if we fail to listen to this channel, like a muscle not exercised, our intuitive abilities will decline.*[4] (Emphasis mine.)

Making that decision to accept the job offer and move to Switzerland was so clearly not what I wanted to do, and deep down, I knew it at the time. But I intellectualized and chose the option that made sense on paper. I learned a huge lesson in trusting my intuition from the whole experience and remind myself of it whenever I have a big decision to make.

From my own lived experience and many, many stories from other highly perceptive people, I believe that we know so much more than we think we do—and learning to trust that knowing is key to living our best lives.

Takeaways

- ☑ Highly perceptive brains are constantly taking in and processing large amounts of data. Making connections between these pieces of information is one of our superpowers—and can also be a source of frustration when (a) we don't realize that we're doing something not everyone can do, (b) others don't understand or agree with us when we know that we know but can't explain how, or (c) we don't learn to trust ourselves and our knowing.

- ☑ Another strength that comes from making all these connections is seeing both the big picture and the details. The flip side of this—the challenges—is a tendency toward perfectionism and a resistance to delegating responsibilities, both of which can negatively affect not only our own ability to be efficient and effective (not to mention our mental health!), but also the learning and development of our team members.

- ☑ Intuition is a gift that all humans are born with and that highly perceptive people seem to have in abundance. Learning to trust it exercises the muscle, which in turn can fine-tune it and lead to better decision-making.

Highly perceptive in the workplace

Kara Peabody, a principal product manager whose colleagues recognize that "if you want a good user experience, (she) can make that happen," attributes her entire career success in tech to being highly perceptive.

When she started out in customer service, Kara's boss noticed her dedication to problem-solving and the way she went above and beyond to serve her customers. Many companies expect customer support professionals to keep calls as short as possible, to maximize the number of calls handled and (ostensibly) the number of customers served. Kara was spending more time on video calls and screen sharing than anyone else on her team—and her customers were happy.

Kara's boss recognized the value she brought to her customers and, by extension, to her own company, and created a new role for her as the technical account point person for their biggest customer, a Fortune 100 corporation. She was empowered to spend as much time as she needed to find the right solutions for their problems. Soon after, supported by all the positive feedback from her customers, she was asked to be the company's first customer success manager.

Then someone on another team noticed her work: "'You talk to a lot of customers, you really know what they want. Could you come over to Product?' That's been my entire career path," Kara told me. "I don't have a degree in product or tech support. It's just listening to people and trying to help them figure out solutions."

Making connections and strategic problem-solving have been key factors in her success, and Kara also credits her empathy: "I think the empathetic part of understanding that when a user or customer is telling me, 'I want this feature,' that's not always what they're asking for, and digging deeper and getting down to what the real problem is. And coming up with a solution for that. Being able to really listen and try to understand their pain."

Speed vs. diligence

For all the success she's had with creating great user experiences, Kara has struggled with being highly perceptive at work.

A different former boss criticized her approach. He told her she needed to spend less time going down rabbit holes. Be less thorough and less perfectionistic. Basically, he wanted her to get shit done—and didn't seem to care much about the details or whether the problem had actually been solved.

This is a common frustration for differently wired people in the workplace; I've heard it from clients and many leaders I've spoken with. I asked one highly perceptive executive who's well respected and loved by her team what, if anything, has held her back, what she's struggled with in her career.

Her reply: "Well, I think I feel slower. Probably because I'm digesting all that information and figuring out what the hell to do with it."

The research agrees. Not only are our brains processing more information per second, but we also have a strong built-in "pause-to-check" system. Different from the emergency "fight, flight, or freeze" response we're all familiar with, the *behavioral inhibition system* (BIS) is a concept developed by British psychologist Jeffrey Alan Gray in his theory of human behavior, along with the *behavioral activation system* (BAS). To oversimplify, Gray theorized that these two systems form the basis of our motivation either toward reward (BAS) or away from punishment or failure (BIS). Elaine Aron, the first psychologist to research and write about highly sensitive people, hypothesizes that HSPs have a stronger-than-usual BIS, which causes many of us to pause to process information.[1]

Highly perceptive people might pause before answering an important question or speaking up in a meeting. Some might appear to hesitate when assessing a new situation or making a decision. It's not usually about fear, or shyness, or even confidence—we want to be effective and efficient and deliver the right response, or whatever seems the most right based on all the information we're digesting and processing.

And sometimes, we take more time because we know, intuitively, that the quick answer isn't the right one, and we're committed to going down the necessary rabbit holes to find it.

There's also a group of highly perceptive folks who don't necessarily take things slowly: the sensation seekers I wrote about in Chapter 1. This group has a stronger behavioral activation system and doesn't come across as cautious or restrained. Although we're still taking in and analyzing large loads of information, we tend to take action quickly. Because our BIS and BAS are both strong, we can move fast and still make fewer mistakes than people with a dominant BAS.[2]

Small talk and being social at work

When highly perceptive people find favorable conditions in their workplace, their conscientiousness, high-quality deliverables, strategic thinking, creativity, and other strengths often place them among the most valuable employees in an organization.[3]

Favorable conditions are the key, though, and in the corporate world today those can seem harder than ever to find or create.

As I mentioned in Chapter 1, 70 percent of HSPs are introverts. And even the extraverted among us aren't usually fans of small talk. It's not that we don't want to be social—it's that the conditions (and the content) matter.

What happens before we even arrive at work matters. A difficult commute, for example, can cause overwhelm at the start of the day, and we might need a few minutes to reset when we get to the office. Clare Kumar, an extravert, describes the commute she had to and from her last corporate job in Toronto:

"The TTC [the subway, run by the Toronto Transit Commission] is dark, noisy, dirty, crowded. Lighting is challenging. Crowded platforms where there's no barrier so you're walking along, and you feel like you might get bumped over the edge onto the tracks. The noise—I mean, just the trains pulling in and out of the subway station making incredible noise—they're not quiet like in Montreal. It's a louder system and it's basically a tiled echo chamber. And we're sitting in 17-inch-wide seats with puffy down jackets in the winter, and in the summer, there was no air conditioning then, and so it becomes a sensory overwhelm, an uncomfortable climate to be in.

"Then you had a lack of an adequate number of cars to take people, so it's crowded inside the cars. You're dealing with all kinds of tensions and now today we're also witnessing a lot more people struggling with mental health issues, drug issues. Safety on the subway has been a thing. Oh, and the breakdowns! And before there were cell phones you were left being unable to communicate if there was a delay. So the whole thing feels like you're disempowered, you're in a toxic environment."

This description brought back so many memories for me. Going to high school in New York City, I sometimes chose to walk three miles downtown to my mother's office if I was meeting her at the end of the day, just to avoid the sensory overwhelm that came with taking the subway or a crowded bus.

It also brought back the streetcars in St. Petersburg, Russia, where I lived for a few months during college. It was 1989, before the fall of the Soviet Union (the city was still Leningrad then). The summer was hot and humid, and there was a very different level of hygiene than I was used to (most people didn't shower every day, used an industrial bar of laundry soap for everything, and weren't familiar with deodorant, which wasn't widely available anyway). Picture a streetcar full of people packed like sardines, dripping with sweat; I can almost smell the body odor just remembering. Completely overwhelming for a sensitive nervous system. (I won't even get into some of the Aeroflot flights I took that year!)

If you're at all sensitive to sound, smells, temperature, lack of personal space, or other people's energy, you won't have to try hard to imagine what it's like to endure all this before you even arrive at work. If it takes everything you have just to survive your morning commute, how do you get through the rest of the day?

Then you get to the office, and a group of coworkers is chatting in the break room about their weekend, sharing every detail of their families' activities.

All you want is to find a few minutes of peace and quiet to get grounded and recharge a bit, so you can take on your day's full schedule of meetings and projects. But if you don't stop and smile and contribute to the conversation, you're judged as standoffish—or worse.

Tricia Livermore, founder and heart-centered coach of Soul Business Advisor LLC and Heartmath-certified mentor, faced this scenario every day: "I'm not a morning person. I come in, I'm trying to acclimate. I'm doing the best that I can. There were some challenges coming into a large, crowded area—I just want my bubble around me. So having to put on a face or pretend to be somebody I'm not, putting on that mask, was very, very challenging for me."

It's challenging for so many highly perceptive people. I vividly remember having to choose between a rock and a hard place: Put the mask on and stay and chat, which takes extra energy and feels inauthentic, or say good morning and keep walking, and hope no one takes it personally or starts whispering about me or excluding me from things.

As Tricia said, we're just trying to acclimate (especially if we're not morning people to begin with—I'm not, either!). I suspect there are more reasons why small talk is harder for us: When we're interested and engaged in a topic, we're all in. When we're not, we'd rather spend our limited time and energy on something we can be interested and engaged in—or at least on the work we're there to do.

A phrase I've used and heard from many other highly perceptive people is, "I have no poker face." My emotion usually shows, and I find it hard to pretend. If a group of people is talking about what they did over the weekend and I'm not only *not* engaged in the conversation but also tired and enervated from my morning commute and thinking about everything I have to get done that day, it'll be challenging for me to look interested.

But none of this is to say that we don't want to be social at work or build relationships with our colleagues—we do! We're just better at it when the conditions are right: when we've been able to recharge, when we've slept well and we're not stressed about an upcoming deadline or meeting, and when there's a topic of conversation that feels meaningful to everyone.

Just being able to have a quieter start to the day was one of the few blessings of the Covid-19 pandemic for people who are highly sensitive or wired differently and were able to work from home.

Physical environments

Another challenge for HSPs and other highly perceptive employees at work is the workplace itself.

The same factors that affected Clare in the Toronto subway can also be a problem in the office: noise, harsh lighting, and an inability to control the temperature (or escape fans, air conditioners, or heaters that are blowing right on you) can cause extreme discomfort or worse. Smells, lack of access to natural light, lack of privacy, and unergonomic, one-size-fits-all desks and chairs can cause all kinds of health problems.

My first full-time job after college was with the San Francisco chapter of a national nonprofit. There were only a few of us, but because we worked privately with clients, we each had our own office. Mine was beautiful, with an exposed brick wall and floor-to-ceiling windows, a large Persian rug, flourishing floor plants, and handsome cherry wood furniture. I guess it could only go downhill from there!

I eventually left for another nonprofit, where the office wasn't quite as nice but was very quiet, and again there were only a few of us. Sometimes I was the only one there, so it was easy to get work done.

Then I entered tech and the world of the open office environment.

At first, again, I was lucky. I worked for a startup, and because of the nature of my work—editing a high volume of daily news articles for inclusion in company profiles—I had to start at 6 a.m. Not ideal (again, not a morning person), but I'd grab a giant muffin and coffee from the little corner bakery and join my other editor colleague, and we worked in silence until others trickled in a few hours later.

Thinking back, I'm amazed I lasted at that job. We edited several hundreds of articles each per day—I think my record was somewhere over 1,200, but I use the term "edited" loosely—and almost never left our stations. Colleagues from customer service and IT would try hard to distract us or make us laugh by sneaking up behind us or waving things over our monitors. Easily distractible as I am, I somehow managed to stick with my mission and get the job done. The company was acquired, and we were all laid off together less than a year after I started, so it's hard to say how much longer I would've lasted.

A few years later, I moved to Seattle to work at Amazon. I was on the team that launched the original Toys site, a special experience that bears little resemblance to today's megastore. While I enjoyed my work, I had a very hard time in the open office environment, which was pretty much a free-for-all. Flying Nerf balls and frisbees and people zooming around on Razor scooters were just the start. Imagine a middle school courtyard during recess, and that might come close.

So when, more than a decade after that, the VP I was interviewing with proudly gave me a tour of the still-under-construction open office I mentioned in the Introduction, I had to hold back a groan. He was so excited about the innovation and collaboration that would magically happen in that giant open space. I was just trying to get an offer, having been laid off (again) several months earlier at another startup, the day I signed the mortgage papers for the condo I was living in at the time. I kept my mouth shut and didn't mention the research that had already been published about the detrimental effects of open-plan offices on many (most?) employees and the fact that the promised innovation and collaboration often didn't happen.

Obviously, I did get the offer, and as I wrote earlier, spent the next two and a half years dealing with the noise, kitchen smells, crazily varying temperatures, harsh lighting, and all kinds of other distractions. The constant sensory overwhelm, combined with the toxicity and my own lack of boundaries and inattention to self-care, all contributed to the burnout I described at the beginning of this book.

Office politics

Another area that can be very hard to navigate for professionals who are wired differently is office politics. Authenticity, transparency, fairness, and justice tend to be core values for us. And since highly sensitive brains are optimized for successful group outcomes, it doesn't even occur to many of us to put our own interests before that of the team. So political maneuvering can take us by surprise, and it puts us (as well as everyone else who isn't directly involved) at a disadvantage.

Sometimes it just frustrates us or pisses us off. As Clare Kumar explained, "I see it, I say it, and I say it directly. I don't play politics, and I have no poker face. So I am not going to be the one to outmaneuver anybody. I'm just going to be like, 'This is what I noticed, and this is what you want to be paying attention to, and that's it.' I don't want to play games. I don't have time to play games. I think it's a waste of time, but I understand that's not how things work all the time."

I couldn't have put it better myself. And although I've separated it out here, office politics can also be a contributing factor to the larger problem of toxic environments.

Toxic environments

In her introduction to *The Canary Code: A Guide to Neurodiversity, Dignity, and Intersectional Belonging at Work*, Ludmila N. Praslova, PhD, writes, "Organizational problems like the lack of fairness, bullying, and toxic cultures impact people with more intense senses and nervous systems before affecting others. Sensitive does not mean broken: it means processing the experience more fully, and intensely, just like birds process the air—the oxygen and the pollutants—more fully."[4]

The "canary in the coal mine" metaphor that Praslova's title references was an actual practice in 20th-century coal mining in the UK: Miners would take canaries underground with them to serve as living carbon monoxide detectors. As she points out, toxic environments may harm the "canaries" first but will ultimately affect everyone in the organization. I highly recommend reading her book for an in-depth look at how organizations can intentionally adopt neuroinclusive systems and practices that create a culture everyone can thrive in.

I suspect every one of us has experience in a work environment that was toxic in some way. A study by Revelio Labs using 2021 data analyzed 34 million online employee profiles to determine the top five reasons for attrition during the Great Resignation. Unsurprisingly, the study found that a toxic work culture "is 10.4 times more likely to contribute to attrition than compensation."[5]

Researchers then studied more than 1.3 million Glassdoor reviews from employees based in the United States to dig deeper into what makes a work culture toxic. They found that five things have the biggest impact and create the most negative views of workplace culture: disrespect, lack of inclusion, unethical activity, cutthroat behavior, and abusiveness.[6]

Looking back at all the companies I worked for over the course of my career, I can count at least one of these factors, if not several, in most of the environments. It's no wonder I was quick to leave so many. Returning to the canary metaphor, I can also count several instances where I left first, and then, within months or a year or two at most, others followed in droves as the toxicity became apparent to those who were not as sensitive to it.

Last year, I had three highly perceptive coaching clients at the same time who were all struggling to navigate different toxic work environments without quitting their jobs.

Each was a seasoned leader, respected in her field. In each case, the cumulative effects of the disrespectful, noninclusive, and abusive behavior, and, in at least one company, cutthroat and unethical practices, were causing extreme stress and affecting the leader's emotional, mental, and sometimes physical health. How could they not?

Two of the women were eventually affected by mass layoffs, which turned out to be the best possible outcome for both. Each told me she felt overwhelmingly relieved; both were fortunate in that their circumstances allowed them to take a little time to rest, recover, and think about next steps.

Characteristically for an HSP, the one who managed a team was initially more concerned for her direct reports than for herself—one of the traits that makes her such a beloved leader and colleague.

At this point, there shouldn't be any surprises about why people with, as Praslova puts it, "more intense senses and nervous systems" are so severely affected by toxic environments:

We perceive subtle signs that not everyone picks up on. We may not know exactly what's going on, but our Spidey senses tell us that something's up. This could be that a particular person doesn't have the organization's best interests at heart, or that something big is on the horizon—like mass layoffs—and the executive team doesn't want productivity to fall prematurely, which might happen if they were to provide a heads-up. In any case, we know, from the energy, from body language, from a lack of communication or other indicators, that something isn't right.

We have a strong moral code. Back to my conversation with Clare about a difference she perceives between HSPs and autistics: My sense is that highly perceptive people may not always feel confident—or safe—enough to speak truth to power, especially earlier in our careers. But when we witness injustice, whether it's a company behaving unethically towards customers or an individual or group of employees being bullied or treated unfairly, it affects us deeply.

Ludmila Praslova, in an article in *Fast Company*, defines moral injury as a "trauma response to witnessing or participating in workplace behaviors that contradict one's moral beliefs in high-stakes situations with the potential of physical, psychological, social, or economic harm to others."[7]

Being party to a transgression of any kind or feeling betrayed by a leader or colleague can result in moral injury, with accompanying feelings of "guilt, shame, anger, grief, anxiety, and disgust. It also often leads to disillusionment in people, particularly in authority figures, and organizations (hence leaving employment in favor of self-employment). Self-loathing, existential, and spiritual crises are also common. Some individuals may develop physical illness or maladaptive behavior (substance abuse, self-isolation)."[8]

We're wired to optimize for successful group outcomes. If we're seeing or sensing activity that suggests that the group can't be successful—unethical or unjust behavior, for example, or impending layoffs—it can be extremely hard for us to continue doing our jobs.

Toxic environments affect us on multiple levels. Not only do they weigh heavily on us and affect our health and well-being (physically and mentally), but they can also be "roadblocks to career advancement." Rachel Kumar, a seasoned product leader, added, "The challenge of being asked to participate in ways that perpetuate the toxic behavior clashes strongly with my moral code, but then I'm not the type of manager or leader that fits their mold."

I'm glad Rachel brought this up; I think we can all relate. We might even feel that we're alone in experiencing this clash and just need to learn how to put up with it, or that we're somehow responsible for fighting the toxicity or protecting others from it all on our own. I've felt all these things at various points in my career. But if or when you find yourself in a(nother) toxic work situation, ask yourself—as I asked the leaders I mentioned above—what is most important here? What would be an ideal outcome for you? And where do your innate integrity and other values rank compared with professional success in this particular environment? You may be the only one looking out for you; when you answer these questions, be aware of any tendency to put your team, your boss, your company, or even your family first.

Solutions that benefit everyone

Many of the challenges in this chapter could be addressed by a combination of inclusive practices and flexible policies in the workplace. For example:

- Sharing—in advance—meeting agendas and specific topics or questions that require input gives team members whose brains process things more deeply extra time to think about what they want to say or how to contribute.

- A lot of stress can be alleviated for everyone when unnecessary meetings are eliminated. Think about the number of back-to-meetings you've attended just to watch PowerPoint presentations where the presenters did nothing more than read the notes in the deck. Allowing team members to work asynchronously and consume information on their own schedules enables larger chunks of focus time. Expensive meeting time can then be used for collaboration.

- Allowing people who must work on-site to commute at less busy times can help prevent sensory overwhelm before they even arrive at the office. Giving employees flexibility and autonomy over their schedule can ease stress over potentially conflicting commitments like dropping off/picking up kids, workouts, classes, etc.

- There are a lot of resources now for creating sensory-friendly spaces, and firms that specialize in designing workplaces that actually work for more people.

- Not everyone has the space to set up a dedicated home office, but those who prefer to work remotely often find that the conditions they can control make the environment more conducive to working than conditions at the office. Empowering employees to work wherever they're most comfortable is likely to result in both higher engagement and higher productivity.

Note that each of these practices offers benefits for everyone in an organization—not only HSPs and neurodivergent employees.

To disclose or not to disclose?

Clients have asked me if they should disclose their trait to their manager or to HR, either to ask for accommodation or simply explain something they're finding challenging. There's no easy answer.

Being highly perceptive isn't a disability. And, unfortunately, some of the stigma around the word sensitivity stems from individuals (who may not even be highly sensitive but who have their own agenda) using it manipulatively as an excuse for special treatment; not wanting to be seen that way at work is a valid concern. If you have a diagnosis or condition that's covered by the Americans with Disabilities Act (ADA) in the United States—ADHD, autism, and dyslexia are three examples—or similar legislation in another country, you might be legally protected from losing your job just for disclosing it, but in many cases your employer is only required to make "reasonable accommodation" that doesn't cause them "undue hardship." These terms are all open to interpretation.

In other words, you need to use your judgment about what you share and with whom. Will any accommodation you might get be worth the potential risks? If you feel safe and believe that your manager or HR partner truly has your best interest at heart, talking with them about what you need to be at *your* best might be a win-win. Their understanding alone could make a difference. If you're not comfortable with it, though, it's a risk you might not want to take. My suggestion: Weigh the best- and worst-case scenarios for disclosing and not disclosing. Consider which outcomes you'd be satisfied with, and which would be deal-breakers.

Takeaways

- ☑ Being highly perceptive in the workplace brings great advantages to the organizations we work for—empathy and understanding customer needs, conscientiousness, and a talent for problem-solving among them.

- ☑ Because of all the extra information our brains are downloading and processing and our built-in "pause-to-check" systems that focus on being thorough and getting things right, some of us may need more time to complete projects or tasks than those whose goal is simply to get shit done.

- ☑ Sensation-seeking HSPs with strong behavioral activation systems can often take action quickly and still make fewer mistakes.

- ☑ People who don't participate in office small talk may be introverts, may not be fully awake in the morning, or may have had a long or rough commute and just need a few minutes of quiet to recharge before interacting. We may be focused on something else. It doesn't mean we never want to socialize, and we shouldn't be judged or penalized for it.

- ☑ Physical environments are another key factor in our ability to succeed at work. Under the right conditions, we can thrive. If we can't find or create those conditions, we're more likely to fail, burn out, or leave.

- ☑ Like canaries in coal mines, those of us who are wired differently are more sensitive to toxic work environments. If we leave first, it's a good indication that there will be a larger exodus to come.

- ☑ Inclusive practices and flexible policies can make an enormous difference—and benefit not only highly sensitive or neurodivergent employees but everyone. Providing options gives all employees some autonomy, which in turn supports engagement and loyalty. It's good for the people and the business.

- ☑ The question of whether to share your trait with a leader or HR is a complicated one; the answer will be specific to you and your situation, and is worth exploring.

6

The highly perceptive leader

"I used to worry that I sometimes came across as a people pleaser or someone who needs consensus in order to drive change and have direction. But I actually need those inputs in order to lead effectively."

Jemma Campbell, cofounder and chief creative officer of creative consultancy Ladyship, shared with me her thoughts on the challenges of being highly perceptive in a leadership role. We talked about the stigma associated with being seen as sensitive—on top of the challenges so many women leaders already face simply by being women in a world still dominated by men.

"I care about perception, because in our industry, in the creative brand and advertising world, for generations, it was always perceived that people who had a very strong point of view, who were very bullish, typically men, were the creative geniuses because they knew instinctively what to do. And they directed with their gut. Whereas I'm considering all the inputs, and I would never think or suggest that I'm better than anybody else on the team.

Even though I have people on the team who are more junior than me, everybody's inputs are valuable and valid.

"Obviously I can make a decision very quickly because I've been doing what I do for several years, but I take my time to think about the inputs. It might slow me down, but at the same time, I'm leading with authenticity, I'm leading with high EQ, and I never want to make a rash decision and then regret it later. Because here's the other thing: They say you only make a first impression once, but I think it's continual. Think about working with your teammates. If you upset somebody, they can hold a grudge for a very long time. You have to be mindful of making mistakes with people from a communication standpoint. And I don't think that style of leadership works anymore anyway, to just shoot from the hip all the time.

"No one should be looking to one person to make all the decisions—it has to be a team effort. I do get bogged down by my own thoughts when I'm competing with men. Some men can often just be like, 'Well, here's what I think,' straight out of the gate. I'm just not that way inclined.

"I think long-term, I am more successful without that style of leadership. But short-term, I wonder if there are certain perceptions of me because I'm a little bit quieter or a little bit softer in my leadership style."

Jemma touched on something we all deal with but don't talk about enough: "For so long, we've been taught to behave like a man. There's a nervousness around presenting yourself as someone with a range of emotions at work because, unfortunately, there are negative connotations with that, right? Like we're weaker or we worry more or we care too much. It's never been a good thing, and again that goes back to what we think strong leadership is. And it's not what I was describing before—it can't be that anymore, it doesn't work. There's too much trauma associated with that."

I think back to experiences I had with female managers who clearly had taken on—consciously or unconsciously—the persona of the strong boss who had everything under control and whose authority was not to be questioned. They showed no emotion and little empathy. They expected their word to be accepted as law, and there wasn't much room for discussion.

As someone who asks a lot of questions, has never believed in doing something a certain way just because it's always been done that way before, and feels that authority (and respect for that authority) should be earned, I frustrated them.

I have more compassion for them now than I had then. Few, if any, of these women had access to the kind of authentic role models I would've liked to have myself—successful women leaders who were completely true to themselves and led in their own way, rather than emulating what they saw all around them.

The struggle for so many women executives, between authenticity and masking,* is very real. I've faced it in my own leadership

---

Psychology Today defines *masking* as "the observable discrepancy between underlying preferences and outward behavior; it may be prompted by wanting to avoid judgment, rejection, and bullying, to make friends or find a romantic partner, or to succeed in [one's] career."[1] Although the term is commonly used in the context of autism or neurodivergence, masking has long been used by individuals and groups outside the dominant culture in any context. Intersectionality makes masking even more complicated: race, gender, and neurodivergence are just three of many factors that can prompt a real or perceived need to modify behavior, appearance, speech, or other aspect of our identity or personality. Some masking is a conscious attempt to blend in or be less visible; sometimes it's an adaptation so ingrained we don't realize we're doing it. We've simply become too adept at observing what's "acceptable" and what's not in the culture we're immersed in.

roles, and failed many times. First, I had very few role models myself. And second, I'm just starting to come to terms with how much I've masked throughout my life, without realizing I was doing it.

Which is one reason I immediately liked Kit Unger, a senior design leader based in the Seattle area. Kit's a beloved leader with a devoted following. Having worked with her, I know why: She has the vision and skills that have earned her her position, but more importantly, Kit leads with empathy, humility, and authenticity.

An example: "Sometimes I would cry at a team meeting and then just be horrified at myself for doing that. But then people would say, 'We love that you're so real with us because it gives us permission to be real.'"

Kit doesn't shy away from the challenges that come with being highly perceptive. She has been called "too sensitive," and is concerned that occasionally she and her team members don't get the serious consideration they deserve. She can be a perfectionist, too.

"I get nervous," Kit admitted, "especially if I perceive that someone is upset or not happy, because I'm an over-the-top people pleaser, which makes it hard to set boundaries. I sometimes take criticism too personally. I want to always be prepared. I have difficulty articulating things that I just know are true because I don't know *how* I know. And then this other thing. This is silly. I don't even know why I'm adding it. Sometimes if we're in workshops and everybody likes music playing, I hate it. I hate it when I'm trying to concentrate on solving a problem. I find it distracting because I want to listen to the song. Turn the music *off*, please."

I so appreciate that she added this, and it's not silly at all. While it may not relate specifically to leadership, it's a common environmental sensitivity issue that affects a lot of people—but so many of us think it's just us and we have to suffer in silence. I can't stand hearing music when I'm trying to focus, either—especially if it has lyrics. I get distracted and can't concentrate on the task. Kit said immediately afterwards that she loves music. I do, too; I have it on in my car all the time. And no one would question the therapeutic benefits of music: it activates many systems in our bodies and brains. But it has to be the right music for the person—and their brain—and for the context. I know a lot of ADHDers, for example, who can't work *without* music. I know just as many people who can't work *with* it. We're all wired a little differently. And a leader who experiences these challenges personally has an advantage: awareness of how important it is to create an environment where individuals' needs are respected and where team members are empowered and encouraged to advocate for themselves.

While acknowledging the frustrations of sensitivity, Kit embraces the many strengths that come with it: "I have loads of empathy and I think that makes me relatable. And I think that has helped me in my career. This curiosity, the love of learning new things. I'm in a perfect field for me because it's ever-changing, and I've got to keep learning new things and I love that. Surrounding myself with really smart people has been a key to my success." Kit also noted that she's a creative problem solver. And a persistent one: When she knows she's on the right track, she doesn't give up.

Other strengths: "I'm decisive; I'm able to get input from a lot of different people with different perspectives and then make a call and trust myself. And trying to see the opposing points of view, being open to that and understanding the business needs, and that I'm paid to move things forward. Helping my bosses know that I know that has helped."

Note the echoes of some of Jemma's comments from the beginning of the chapter. Two highly perceptive women executives in different but related industries who've succeeded in a new paradigm—leading with empathy and authenticity.

More struggles and strengths of highly perceptive women leaders

As I've tried to show throughout this book, the superpowers and the challenges of high sensory perception are two sides of the same coin. And I use that metaphor consciously. As someone who's lived with all of them, I can't and won't make light of the things we struggle with. That said, there's so much good here—so much value. I'd rather have the coin than not.

My hope is that by the end of the book, if you are highly perceptive and have struggled with the challenges, you're ready to embrace and celebrate your superpowers and the things that make you uniquely you.

Another note: I've specified women leaders in the section header because, as I mentioned earlier, most of my clients are women, and for many reasons, it's been easier to find women leaders who identify with the trait and are willing to be interviewed. Highly perceptive male (and gender-fluid and nonbinary) leaders do exist, face many of the same challenges, and have the same strengths. There are some differences too. That might be a topic for another book!

Perfectionism and delegating

I mentioned that I call myself a "recovering perfectionist," as do a lot of highly perceptive people I know. Intellectually, I understand that most people aren't paying as much attention to the details as I am. I get that "perfect is the enemy of good" and that it's often better to get something done than nothing.

That said, I'm wired for details. I perceive the slightest nuances in tone, hue and shade. So if something feels off to me, I know it'll feel off to a large part of my audience—other highly perceptive people.

I still spend too long fiddling with details in my writing and on my website. But there are areas where I've learned to give up some control. My earliest YouTube videos are very low quality; I didn't know anything about video editing or production and didn't have the budget to hire a pro to help me. I rerecorded each one many times, because most are unscripted, and although I made notes to myself, I often went off-track or just didn't like the way it came out. But I realized that it was better to get something out than nothing at all, and I learned by doing. (I'm very much still learning—creating and editing videos will never be my zone of genius. And I've learned to be ok with that.)

I bring this topic up again here because it comes up in so many conversations with highly perceptive leaders: They want things to be perfect. But wanting things to be perfect can make it hard to trust other people to carry out your vision—it makes delegating tricky. And one of the most important things leaders have to learn is how and when to delegate.

Minette Norman and I both shared our challenges with learning to delegate. To me, it just seemed more efficient to do things myself—easier and faster than explaining everything to someone else when I already had the context. And when I knew I could do it exactly the way I wanted it done.

But managing people and teams this way is self-defeating. Teams are hired when there's too much for one person to do and when additional or specialized skill sets are needed. In my case, I'd hired everyone on the team for their skill and experience. My role was to make strategic decisions and lead the team to contribute to the product in ways that made everyone successful, including both our customers and the team members themselves. I couldn't do any of those things well if I were buried in the details and didn't trust my team members to do good work—and help them learn and develop their own skills. It was an important (and very painful, at times) part of my own growth journey as a leader, and I wish I'd had a coach or mentor to help make it a little less painful.

One more thing. You've heard the phrase, "can't see the forest for the trees"? Even though many of us are gifted at being able to see both, we can sometimes get a little too fascinated by the individual trees and lose sight of the beauty of the forest.

I recently asked a friend, a brand strategist, to look at my website. I wasn't happy with it. There were a few areas I knew I needed to work on but couldn't figure out what to do with. My friend slowly and empathetically critiqued every part of the site, until I realized it was pretty much a hot mess. (My words, not hers.) I'd spent so much time on the details that it had grown organically into something that no longer served prospective clients well, and it took getting an outside perspective to see it. I finally hired an experienced professional designer. Leaving it to an expert was the best thing I could possibly have done, and not only am I happier with my site now, it's garnered compliments from several highly perceptive leaders who don't say things they don't mean.

We all have our zones of genius—and most of us have far too much to do in general. We set ourselves and others up for success when we focus on our strengths and delegate the other things on our list to the people who can do them most effectively.

Receiving feedback

Kit Unger mentioned that she "sometimes takes criticism too personally." This is another recurring theme for most of the highly perceptive leaders I interviewed for the book and those I talk with every day. (And yup, my hand is raised too.)

This isn't particularly surprising, as we're so often perfectionists, recovering or not. We want to do and be our best, at all times and in all things. Also unsurprisingly, it's not about ego. Sure, there's ego involved. We're human. But what I hear over and over again is "I want to be the best I can be for my company," or my team, or my kids. We want to succeed because we want success for them. And we want to leave the world a better place than we found it.

Alecia Page, a leader in workplace culture, employee engagement, and DEI, got feedback early in her career that she had great skills and knowledge but needed to be warmer and friendlier. She was contributing to conversations at a leadership level, but missed out on promotions because she didn't "play the political game"— she spoke her truth and it pissed some people off. She was told she came across as a know-it-all when she had timely information and wanted to help.

"As I got older," Alecia told me, "I made it a point to surround myself with people who I saw were good at that part of it and ask them, 'Why do you think that this leader is so resistant to me,' or, 'Why can't I get invited to this meeting, even though I have a lot to contribute?' And anytime someone gave me feedback, if I felt personal resistance to it, I was like, 'Listen, Self, *your goal is to get to a higher level so that you can make a higher impact so that the working world doesn't look like this anymore.* And if that means you have to take it on the chin for right now, then you find a way to grin and bear it.'

"And that's a lot of what my career is now," Alecia continued. "There are a lot of moments when I feel myself having that internal reaction to something that's like, this isn't fair, this isn't okay, or this is very uncomfortable to have to work in this way. The bigger goal is that I want to make an impact. And I know now this is what these kinds of people expect from me. So I'll do what I have to do to get there and then change the rules later."

When I asked Jemma Campbell what she thought had been key to her success, she talked about learning how to receive feedback, and to keep it in perspective:

"I take feedback seriously. Even if it's coming from a place that is unwarranted, I will still sit with it. Even if it's someone's opinion and it's not formal feedback, I sit with it, whether I agree with it or not. And I still make improvements from that feedback. Quite often I find that I've had negative feedback that is actually somebody else projecting or attacking me to protect themselves. But I refuse to ignore that feedback. There's always something in it that I can use to improve myself."

It's so easy to forget that feedback is often subjective and can reflect more on the giver than the receiver, unless it's gathered, compiled and delivered thoughtfully and intentionally. Jemma has a few tips for those of us who find it hard to take feedback gracefully:

- **Seek counsel from trusted peers and from your boss, if you have a good relationship.** And be honest with them. In the past, she's shared that she got some feedback and wanted to talk about it and get their perspective. "I think it's important to not hold on to it as if it's shameful but talk about it openly and honestly."
- **If what you've been told isn't helpful or clear, ask questions.** As Jemma was told by a successful woman she looks up to: "Consider what was said. Consider the context. You need actionable input. If you're not getting that, then you need to hold them accountable so that they're giving you constructive feedback."
- **Separate yourself from your role.** "This is not an attack on you as a person. It's about you as you are in your role. This is the role you perform. That is the feedback that you're getting. So I try to mindfully uncouple the two."

It's never been easy for Minette Norman to accept feedback, but she's come to terms with it: "People say feedback is a gift. Well, maybe not for the more sensitive of us. But I can stop obsessing about it more quickly than I used to. Now I just ask myself some good questions like, 'What is this bringing up for you? What stories are you telling yourself and are you going to move on?'"

She commented that she's been working with someone who actively solicits hard feedback, and that she herself isn't like that at all. But she's gotten better at handling it. And occasionally, even welcoming it: "There were moments when I got feedback I was so grateful for. And this was when I was really maturing through the years as a leader. I remember when my staff members gave me some feedback once about my not being tough enough in terms of holding them accountable. That was a total blind spot for me. And I was so grateful to hear it. It didn't make me bristle, and it didn't make me feel bad. It was just like, 'Aha.'

"And I think," Minette concluded, "maybe the difference in how I responded to different kinds of feedback is that something I was utterly unaware of felt like a gift. Whereas something that I knew about myself and already felt bad about, that was harder to hear."

Echoing the theme of personal growth, after Kit made the comment about taking criticism personally, she added, "I strongly believe feedback is crucial to growth, and I accept it wholeheartedly when I know the person giving it actually cares about me as a person and my growth."

Giving feedback—and not taking on others' emotions

Delivering feedback can be as hard for highly perceptive leaders as receiving it, for a few reasons.

First, our combination of empathy and conscientiousness usually means that we put a lot of time, thought, and energy into what we're going to say. When I was leading teams and had to give feedback, I would sometimes rehearse whole conversations in my head.

Another leader shared, "I get nervous even thinking about my one-on-ones because I always want to be prepared. I want to know, what are they going to ask? And I need time to process things, figure out how to articulate what I want to say. To me, communication needs to be designed. I wish more people took the time to plan out what they want to say and then said it succinctly and clearly, because I think the world would be a better place."

When you're sensitive to others' feelings, it can be hard to keep your own emotions out of it.

As a people manager and leader, Minette struggled with this. "When someone else was upset, it was very easy for me to take that on, to absorb their emotions. For example, I'm having a one-on-one with one of my staff members. They're crying. For me, what often happens is that you cry, I cry, right? So the challenge was for me not to be swept away in their emotions or their challenges and to be able to maintain the leadership persona while still empathizing and caring."

This particular challenge can determine an entire career path—and potentially color the perceptions of those who make decisions about promotions. A leader who reports to the CEO but doesn't have direct reports commented:

"I don't want to be in management because I don't want to have that conversation—like putting someone on a PIP [performance improvement plan], for example. And I wonder if people get stuck at a certain point because it's hard for them to have those hard conversations."

While having hard conversations is a skill we could all improve, this dilemma she describes is something to think about if your company doesn't offer parallel paths and opportunities for senior individual contributors versus people managers. If you're a highly perceptive leader who knows you don't want to manage people, your options for career advancement may be very limited. Keep your values and goals in mind when you're faced with hard career-related decisions. And if you're in HR or People Operations, consider creating alternative career paths to people management for high achievers who can deliver value to the organization in other ways.

Driving change

A recurring theme in the highly perceptive leadership model that's come up a few times in this chapter is being willing to challenge the status quo and not take no for an answer.

For Minette, this "was fundamental to my success. I was willing to be bold about driving change, and not just incremental change but major change. That's how I went from being an individual manager to a senior manager to taking over a department to being a VP, because I was unwilling to accept that this is the way we do things."

While this commitment to driving change is inarguably a strength, it can also lead to burnout if the leader faces too many obstacles without accompanying successes or doesn't have enough support. We'll get into this further in the next chapter.

More keys to success

Back to the coin with two sides: It might feel like the obstacles to great leadership are insurmountable for people who are more sensitive and perceptive than most. But as I hope the highly respected and well-liked leaders in this chapter and throughout the book show, harnessing your superpowers will lead the way.

I asked a couple of these leaders for advice for other highly perceptive folks looking to enter or advance in a leadership role. Here's what they shared.

From Kit: "Learn to honor your intuition. And take really good care of yourself. Because when you're like us, it's easy to *not* take care of yourself. So make yourself a priority, and stay positive. And because we feel things deeply, surround yourself with the things that you feel deeply good about. Hiking, art, animals, nature, whatever helps you stay positive.

"Pay more attention to things that are validating," Kit added, "and like my husband's always saying to me, be yourself. Just be yourself and learn to like yourself and honor yourself."

And from Minette: "Find what feels right to you. People are going to tell you, you must do this, you must *not* do this, you must speak this way, you must lower your voice, or whatever it is that we tell women. I think you have to be yourself. Don't try to put on a persona that isn't you because, first of all, you can't sustain it; it will exhaust you; it will burn you out. You have to be true to you, and you are also operating in a world that is not fair and where there's not a level playing field. So you will have to play some of the games and some of the politics, but don't let it compromise who you are so that you can get up every day and say, I am living my values, to the degree it's possible in corporate America. I am not compromising my being, my soul. Or my heart.

"All the other things that people will tell you, take them with a big grain of salt. And if this feels right to you and is helpful advice, take it. If it feels like, 'I don't buy into that,' then discard it completely. I got tons of advice, and some of it was helpful and some of it I wasn't interested in. So be true to yourself. Find your voice. It's really important that we find our voice and that it doesn't sound like someone else's."

Takeaways

- ✓ Highly perceptive women leaders most often mention two attributes that have been foundational to their career success: empathy and authenticity.
- ✓ Moving beyond perfectionism and learning to delegate are critical to upleveling leadership skills and establishing executive presence.
- ✓ Giving and receiving feedback can be particularly challenging for highly perceptive leaders. When giving it, prepare what you want to say in advance, including responses to potential questions, and try not to let your own emotions get in the way. On the receiving end, listen with an open mind and focus on what feels real, actionable, and relevant to your role, rather than personal criticism.
- ✓ Many of us are here to challenge the status quo and drive change. Trust your intuition and don't take no for an answer.
- ✓ Take care of yourself, find your voice, and be yourself.

7

Burnout

"I genuinely believe that it's the highly sensitive people in the world who are the changemakers, the change leaders who are in tune with what the world senses and needs. We need to take care of the people who are taking care of the world, right? And we're not doing a very good job with that."

Amy Wilson, founder of the Empathy Action Lab and Healing for Work and author of *Empathy for Change: How to Create a More Understanding World* (New Degree Press, 2021), identifies as an HSP. In one of her many roles, she leads workshops on burnout first aid. I was curious about what had led her to this.

In 2010, Amy was working in management consulting, on a team of five that was tasked with building a culture of innovation at a hundred-year-old company. Within a year of joining the firm, she'd been asked to lead the work.

Surrounded by people with Ivy League degrees and MBAs from Harvard and Stanford, Amy faced impostor syndrome. To both differentiate herself and show she belonged, she decided that she'd become a better executor than everyone else. So she sacrificed her personal life—and quality of life—and worked around the clock. Putting in 80- and 100-hour weeks meant that she was executing better than everyone else—Amy was known as the plate spinner, for her ability to keep all the moving pieces up the air—but she wasn't getting promoted or recognized for her work.

At one point, her team members all took the Gallup Strengths-Finder test to get to know each other a little better. Amy's top strength was empathy.

"I remember in that moment reading it and thinking this makes sense, but I don't think the people around me feel this. I am different from everybody around me, and I'm in management consulting. They don't care about me. They don't care about what I'm doing.

"Fast-forward to about a year and a half later. Everybody, my manager, all the people around me, were dropping like flies because they were burned out. I kept going. I shut off my emotions and just kept being this workhorse. I was numbed out, not feeling my body. I would wake up in the morning and go straight to work. I worked from home, but I'd go until one or two in the morning, rarely eat, only get up to go to the bathroom. That was my life.

"And one day one of my managers asked, 'Hey Amy, you're acting erratic—are you ok?'

"That was the first time anybody'd asked me if I was ok. And I said, 'I'm not ok and I'm struggling,' and then I literally lay in the fetal position for hours and just cried. After that I knew I needed to stop.

"I'd hit bottom. From that point forward I changed everything. I stopped working those long hours; I said I wanted to be pivoted back out to a client site and do product management work, which I was learning about. So I was very clear, I'm now putting boundaries on myself."

A couple of years later, Amy was working in the US government as the director of Innovation.gov, building, among other things, a community called the Better Government Movement that grew to nearly 5,000 members in a short time.

She recalled, "One of the things I found in that movement was that people who are pushing up against a system that doesn't work for most are sometimes going through a lot of mental health challenges. And you have to take care of yourself so that you can keep making those changes happen."

People like this—change agents—are labeled disruptors, she says, and while some people look at bringing in new ideas as a positive thing, leadership doesn't always see it that way. The results can be very negative.

"They see you as something to be stopped. And I saw very early on in that experience that people were burned out from pushing against the system, which was the federal government."

So Amy created a support group for change leaders during the first Trump administration.

"The work I was doing was not really favored in that administration. It's an open, participatory, and peer-driven work, which is what I was studying in the Obama administration and trying to bring into that government, creating government for the people and by the people.

"Around this time, I was told, 'You work for me and you work for this president, and you're thinking of everything wrong.' And I was fired from my job. Innovation.gov was taken down and destroyed. And they told me not to convene the movement again.

There were threats. There was a lot going on. That experience is what led me to write my book around empathy for change.

"After all that happened, I decided to take a sabbatical so I could take care of myself and heal from the trauma of everything. Thankfully, that was a luxury that I had prepared for because I knew I was heading towards burnout again."

Masking and burnout

There's a lot to process in both of these cautionary tales. I heard a few parallels with my own severe burnout story when listening to Amy's: a corporate leadership role, surrounded by smart colleagues, sacrificing quality of life and working crazy hours, and taking pride in being known as "the plate spinner." (In my case, having worked at Boeing many years earlier, I liked the image of an air traffic controller.)

Like Amy, I was also trying to create change, at a 160-year-old company that was going through the motions of modernizing but couldn't quite commit. There were competing cultures (in multiple senses of the word) and strong resistance to new ideas—despite the fact that our business unit had been established in San Francisco, far from the company's US headquarters, specifically to draw from the region's tech-savvy talent. The constant tension between what we in San Francisco knew needed to be done and what HQ in the Midwest would approve was exhausting on its own. It felt like an ongoing uphill battle.

A crucial difference between her stories and mine, though, is that Amy was doing work she believed in and was inspired by. I was doing a job I'd taken to pay the bills. And I was masking.

Masking is a term I've known for several years and heard used in specific contexts. Code-switching, shifting from one language or dialect to another to suit a particular social or cultural context or setting, is a kind of masking when it's done to fit in or to avoid being called out. "Don't Ask, Don't Tell" was a policy that required LGBTQIA+ military service members in the US to hide their sexual orientation or risk dismissal: They had to mask to remain in the service. Masking can apply to physical appearance, too; Black women who've been forced to hide or change the natural texture or style of their hair to conform to White standards are masking. I learned about masking in the context of neurodiversity only recently—and still have a lot to learn.

Surprisingly, I had no idea how much I've been masking all my life. As I wrote earlier, masking can be conscious or not. Karen Renee Halseth talked in Chapter 1 about becoming a watcher out of necessity, almost as a protective shield. I clearly remember observing both the adults and the kids around me at different times—how they dressed, how they interacted. I noticed everything, and I guess I was storing it all away.

I've written about being an odd kid and embracing my weirdness. And I did, to a point. I've never tried to dress or look like other girls or women I know; I always had my own style and stood by it, even when it was... unusual. Like the middle school years when my entire wardrobe was burgundy and gray. Easy to mix and match (and not be too visible).

But I'm very aware, now, of how much time I've spent masking in small ways. Learning how to "do" small talk even though I've never enjoyed it, because it's the socially acceptable way to behave. Smiling in social and professional situations when I don't always feel like smiling but know it's expected.

I remember classmates and colleagues assuming I was feeling a certain way when I wasn't. I've always been intense, but people sometimes thought I was upset or angry when I was just pensive, which concerned me. So now—for as long as I can remember, anyway—I'm hyper-aware of my facial expressions and tone of voice and how I'm coming across. There are still very few people in my life with whom I let my guard down completely.

It occurs to me as I write this chapter that this is one area where I have definite people-pleasing tendencies—even if the ultimate goal is not necessarily to please others but simply to not stand out. Masking is a form of people-pleasing when its purpose is to make other people more comfortable, or less uncomfortable. (I want to make a critical distinction here: when people mask out of fear for their physical or psychological safety, it's not about people-pleasing.)

In either case, it's exhausting. I recognize now that my burnout was caused just as much by trying, too hard and for too long, to be someone I wasn't as by taking on too much, focusing on too many details, and forgetting to include both grace and joy in my life.

The costs of masking

Kalen Cobb, the social worker and therapist we met in Chapter 2, describes herself as "a marginalized, high-achieving, high-masking person," and "former gifted kid." I asked Kalen what masking means to her.

"High masking means appearing as though everything is fine. 'I'm fine. I don't need anything. Don't worry about me.' And that has shown up in school and even in relationships. To this day, sometimes I find I'm distancing myself from others, in fear of being too much, in fear of needing space. I need spaciousness, time for transition. I cannot go from meeting to meeting. I need clarity. I need to know, when you say this on the syllabus, what exactly does it mean? How creative can I get with this? And it's that questioning nature that I think can often rub folks the wrong way, especially when it comes from someone with a marginalized identity."

Kalen told me about a college professor who she felt was visibly frustrated with her for asking clarifying questions and coming to his office hours—she felt he wanted her to stop asking questions and just do the assignment.

"So over the years," Kalen told me, "I've learned that it's my responsibility to wrestle with the question. It's my responsibility to adjust for people's discomfort."

At this point, Kalen drew her arms in tightly. "As you can see, I'm making these movements that are like trying to fit into a space that's way too small for the person I am. And the person that I was created to be. And that is really what high masking means to me—trying to fit into these small spaces that are not meant for me."

When I asked what masking had cost Kalen, she got emotional.

"It has often cost me relationships. When I'm saying I'm contorting myself, I'm closing not only myself off to the true version of me, but other folks as well. I think back to friendships that I had in college where I tried so hard to be this person that I wasn't. I contorted myself and then transformed this into resentment or anger towards those who were just trying to be there, to be supportive.

"Again, realizing that people have not asked me to contort myself, but I've been so accustomed to doing that, that in relationships I've distanced myself and manufactured this loneliness."

I got a little emotional myself just listening to her, my empathy in overdrive as I thought back to some lost relationships of my own.

Kalen added that there's also an intersectional piece to masking: "I think the more marginalized identities you have, the greater the masking has to be in order to make this place work for you. . . . As your marginalized identities add up, the need to mask and the toll of masking just continue to weigh."

Which brings us back to burnout.

During and after college, Kalen was, in her words, "a very depressed human. And I think it really did not occur to me until the beginning of the pandemic that I had been running in a state of burnout for at least the last five years."

She told me that being a high achiever who tried to do everything and not need anyone "weighs on the soul." I can relate. I felt like she could have been describing me in college too.

"And when you are contorting yourself to fit into these spaces," she continued, "to not make others uncomfortable, to grapple with the questions with yourself, to not invite others into the conversation, that is a very tiring process. And for me, the burnout caused by existing in a version that was not my true and authentic self coincided with a deep depression."

Kalen described work she did with her own therapist during the pandemic, and a key realization she came to: "This life that I am on track to create is not something that I want. It's just not sustainable and it will continue this deep burnout. It will continue this depression, this despair, this misalignment. I feel like that really is what burnout is. It's a misalignment. We've been misaligned for so long that it results in a depletion of the self, a disconnect from the true self."

Frighteningly, in her client work she's seeing this fatigue and misalignment in children as young as 11. "What are we doing in our culture," she asked, "that an 11- or 12-year-old is already so deeply tired, so disconnected from themselves?"

Lack of self-awareness and burnout

Burnout recovery coach Mollie Isaacks has written about her own ongoing healing journey. She shared her burnout story with me.

The background: Mollie grew up not understanding that she was highly sensitive or why she faced so many of the challenges that highly sensitive kids face. Not understanding why she felt things so personally, or struggled in so-called friendships where others weren't invested. And this lack of understanding continued into her adult life and through many years in corporate roles, despite being smart and a high achiever.

But then a lifetime of not paying attention to herself and her needs caught up with her: "I was at LinkedIn working with a great team of people, and we had the pandemic. And we had change, and we had change, and we had change. And people looked at me like, 'What's wrong with you?' Well, I went through reorgs twice, and I had four managers in one year. I'm suffering from a whole lot of change, and I don't understand what's going on."

At the same time, Mollie was taking a coaching program at UC Davis. In the program, she was told she needed to learn about self-awareness. That was a wakeup call.

"That started my journey into understanding what was happening, and the more I understood, the worse I got, because I was still in that toxic stew of change. Of lack of compassion. Through this whole series of events, I went from holding my own, being ok, to total burnout, to 'I don't even know how to do my job anymore. I've lost all my self-confidence. I've lost all my cognitive abilities. I'm working 12 hours a day. I'm getting up at seven in the morning. I'm not eating until two or three in the afternoon some days because I have meetings from seven until two. I'm skipping lunches. I'm not exercising.' And these things just got worse as the pandemic continued."

Then, in her words, "everything just crashed."

Mollie described the crash: "I could not function. My brain didn't work. I was at urgent care on a Saturday and asked for a doctor's note. They ran blood tests and found out I had diabetes. I had other stuff I had to deal with. So not only had I burned out, I'd also severely impacted my health in chronic ways as a result of the behaviors that led up to the burnout.

"When I say everything crashed, to me, it felt like the whole world caved in. My health caved in, my job caved in, my brain caved in. My whole mind was just stuck. It couldn't process all the stuff that was happening."

Like Amy's and Kalen's burnout stories, Mollie's was both hard to hear and so relatable. I know exactly what those crazy years were like—working 12-hour days with a schedule so packed with meetings that there's no time to eat, having four different managers in a year. And just trying to power through.

I also still remember what it felt like when my health and my brain caved in, and I just wasn't processing anything properly anymore.

Neurodivergent burnout

Amy, who leads workshops on burnout first aid, says we live in a "burnout world." Everyone's talking about it, and everyone seems to have experienced it, many of us more than once. But, she points out, your healthcare provider won't find burnout in the DSM, so they can't diagnose you.

I hadn't read or heard much (if anything) about burnout in 2014 when I quit and moved to Peru. I don't think it was any less prevalent then, since I now recognize that I'd been burned out before, as far back as college. But I know I spent a lot less time on social media in the years leading up to my realization of it, and people around me weren't talking about it. Now, in any case, people are discussing it, there's research on it, and we're more aware of the signs and symptoms.

It can still be tricky to recognize burnout because it can look different for everyone, and people who've experienced it in the past can experience it differently the next time.

To complicate things, there are different types of burnout. Although it's not in the DSM, burnout is now included in the *International Classification of Diseases* (ICD), developed and maintained by the World Health Organization (WHO). The WHO classified burnout in the 10th revision of the ICD as an occupational phenomenon and refined its definition in the ICD-11 in 2022:

> Burnout is a syndrome conceptualized as resulting from chronic workplace stress that has not been successfully managed. It is characterised by three dimensions: 1) feelings of energy depletion or exhaustion; 2) increased mental distance from one's job, or feelings of negativism or cynicism related to one's job; and 3) a sense of ineffectiveness and lack of accomplishment. Burnout refers specifically to phenomena in the occupational context and should not be applied to describe experiences in other areas of life.[1]

Then there's neurodivergent burnout, which has additional causes and can extend to every part of life—not just work. It can take weeks, months, or even years, as in my case, to recover from severe neurodivergent burnout.[2]

In 2020, researcher Dora Raymaker, PhD, defined autistic burnout as "a syndrome conceptualized as resulting from chronic life stress and a mismatch of expectations and abilities without adequate supports. It is characterized by pervasive, long-term (typically 3+ months) exhaustion, loss of function, and reduced tolerance to stimulus."[3] An article in *Medical News Today* notes that there are distinguishing characteristics of both autistic and ADHD burnout, now both more commonly known as neurodivergent burnout.[4]

A blog post on the unique experience of neurodivergent burnout by UK-based neurodiversity consultancy Creased Puddle put it succinctly:[5]

Chronic stress + expectation + masking − adjustments or support = neurodivergent burnout

To break this down, chronic stress is often considered the root cause of neurotypical burnout. When we add in factors such as the need to mask, trying to meet expectations that are unreasonable or don't take our differences into account, dismissal of neurodivergent lived experience, a lack of boundaries, and innate sensory sensitivities that can lead to overwhelm even when the other factors aren't present, we have a perfect recipe for neurodivergent burnout.[6]

What are the signs of neurodivergent burnout?

Common signs to look for in yourself or someone else include:

- Fatigue or exhaustion
- Low energy; difficulty recharging
- General feeling of numbness
- Loss of interest in things that are usually inspiring or motivating
- Lack of empathy or compassion
- No sense of humor around things you/they would've found funny before
- Frequent irritability, anger, atypical cynicism, or bad moods
- Getting sick a lot or developing new, chronic health conditions
- Increased sensory/environmental sensitivity
- Increased meltdowns or shutdowns
- Loss of skills
- Executive function challenges (e.g., problems with memory or organization)
- Withdrawal from normal social interaction
- Difficulty with basic hygiene and other activities of daily life
- Inability to mask or act "as expected"

Some of the people in Amy's community have described burnout in ways we can probably all relate to:

"Burnout is an elevator with just a down button."

"It's like the Sunday scaries. On Sunday, you're like, 'I don't want to go back to this.'"

"It's a flower that's stopped growing."

Amy added, "Burnout is a system that no longer works for us."

While I agree that it's a systemic problem, I'd argue that the system never worked for many of us. We just contorted ourselves into pretzels to fit in as best we could. Until we couldn't any longer.

Near the end of our conversation, Amy said, "We need to create systems in our life so that we can counteract the systemic force of the world. And we have to build the power within ourselves. That's a big part of our work—building the power within ourselves to step into that role and not be afraid to take those steps."

As a changemaker working with other changemakers, Amy focuses on systems. To be able to challenge the status quo and create systemic change in the world, we have to start by creating systems in our own lives that work for us, support us, reenergize us when we're depleted—or, better, before we get there. How do we create those systems and build that power within ourselves? We start by setting, communicating and enforcing our own boundaries, and practicing self-care, which is the focus of the next chapter.

Takeaways

- ☑ There are a lot of paths that lead to burnout. Leading a fight for change against an entrenched and unjust system is one. As a lot of highly perceptive people are passionate about justice in all its forms, it follows that those of us who are change makers are more vulnerable to burnout.
- ☑ Another route to burnout for high achievers is just to keep on powering through, as we're so used to doing, because if we don't, who will?
- ☑ Masking, whether consciously or unconsciously, takes a huge toll. And intersectionality adds weight: As Kalen pointed out, the more marginalized identities we have, the greater the perceived need to mask and the heavier our mask becomes.
- ☑ Wearing those masks continually and trying to conform to unrealistic expectations without support or accommodation can lead to neurodivergent burnout, which researchers now recognize as a syndrome that's distinct from neurotypical burnout.
- ☑ Everyone experiences burnout differently—whether neurodivergent or neurotypical—and the same person can feel and show it differently at different times. But there are some common signs to help us recognize it.
- ☑ Preventing burnout starts with boundaries, self-awareness, and self-care.

8

Redefining self-care

I was 27 years old when I took my first—and only—all-inclusive vacation. I'd traveled extensively and lived abroad a few times already but was tired of doing it all on my own. I didn't have a partner to travel with, and friends either couldn't take time off or had travel plans with partners or spouses.

I was also just plain exhausted. Working for the tech startup where I started at 6 a.m. and "edited" hundreds of articles a day, I should have been able to end my workday at 3 p.m. But my hyper-conscientiousness made that close to impossible—how could I leave in the middle of the afternoon when all my colleagues were still working and there was plenty of work still to do? This, my first job in tech, was also where I started to work crazy hours, and I was definitely a little burned out.

I decided to try an all-inclusive package. I researched outfitters and destinations. There were plenty of options, but most were either too expensive or for longer than I could take off work.

Finally, I discovered Wild Woman Adventures, a small woman-owned travel company based in the Bay Area, where I lived, that catered to women traveling on their own (sadly, the company closed a few years later). They offered a trip to Mexico, where I hadn't been, that fit my budget and my vacation allowance. The timing was perfect. I was in.

It turned out to be a wonderful experience. I'd been concerned about a big group, which isn't my thing, but there were only three of us: the trip leader; the other tour member, who, coincidentally, also happened to be an editor working in tech; and me. We clicked right away, and since we were close in age and had a lot in common, everyone we encountered assumed we were either sisters or girlfriends traveling together.

The small resort was beautiful. The food was fresh and made with care. We kayaked, rode horses on the beach, swam, hung out at the pool's swim-up bar, and celebrated Día de los Muertos with a costume party, where a flirty staff member dressed up in a bedsheet toga as Mark Antony to my Cleopatra.

I got plenty of sleep and a lot more exercise than usual. We laughed for a week. I was completely taken care of—no need to think about or plan anything. I didn't even have to carry my own suitcase. It felt absolutely luxurious.

So why have I never done anything like that again?

Don't get me wrong—I take time off. And unlike so many of the leaders I know and work with, I do (usually) leave work behind. Even when I can't afford to go far away or take a lot of time, I try to take short breaks—even a day or two—every few months. I need the change of scenery and break in routine for my sanity.

But until recently, I tended to make things harder for myself than necessary. I'd create complicated itineraries or choose off-the-beaten-path places that weren't easy to get to. And, as I've heard often from other coaches and healers, I (still) need to learn to receive.

It was hard for me to be catered to for a week. And although I was paying for all the services and grateful to the staff, I felt guilty at times. At home, I lived alone; there was no one to share responsibilities with, so I did everything. I was unused to being taken care of, and, even more, unused to relaxing for so many days.

Many of the leaders I work with tell me they can relate to this: They're the ones taking care of others—not being taken of themselves. Many have partners and kids and do a lot (if not the bulk) of the work at home caring for the family. Some are caregivers for aging parents or siblings or other family members who need support. Almost all find it hard to prioritize themselves. Whether that means taking time off alone or for something they want to do (as opposed to for their families or partners), or investing in themselves, personally or professionally, they're extremely reluctant.

As I've mentioned more than once, highly sensitive brains are wired to favor successful group outcomes—and family's a big one—not to put themselves first. But we have to find balance: Putting everything and everyone else first all the time can only lead to negative outcomes, and burnout is only one example.

Every time you fly you watch a flight attendant or listen to a recorded voice reminding you, in case of an emergency, to put your own oxygen mask on first before helping those you're traveling with. There's a reason for that. If you don't get the oxygen you need, you won't be capable of helping anyone else.

What does this mean for a population that almost always puts others' needs first? It means we need to redefine self-care.

A lot of people think of self-care as things they can't afford. I won't pretend money doesn't help; a good massage therapist is worth their weight in gold. But taking care of yourself starts with something a lot simpler and, more importantly, free: listening to your body, mind, and soul, and giving them what they need.

Self-care doesn't have to cost anything but time—and the costs of *not* giving yourself that time are far higher. If you're not convinced, I highly recommend reading either *When the Body Says No: The Cost of Hidden Stress* or *The Myth of Normal: Trauma, Illness and Healing in a Toxic Culture* by Gabor Maté. Dr. Maté has researched and written extensively about the connections between severe illness and the constant repression of emotions, needs, and desires. Many of the patients in his case studies sound like textbook HSPs.

So, besides all-inclusive vacations and massages, what does self-care look like?

Looking at our health holistically means ensuring that we take care of every aspect of ourselves: physical, emotional, mental, and spiritual. We're whole, complex beings. In general, when one area needs support, it affects other areas. And when we're healthy and thriving in one area, we tend to thrive in all.

Following are some of the many ways we can take better care of ourselves.

Get more, and better, sleep

We're often told that adults need eight hours of sleep per night for optimal health. But there are a lot of factors that combine to determine how much sleep we really need, including age, quality of sleep, and overall health. And those of us who are wired differently may need more than others.[1]

It makes sense. Our brains are always on. Our nervous systems are on high alert more often than most. Our bodies and our brains both need rest.

Context matters too. If we spend much of our time in a quiet, low-stress environment under conditions of our own choosing, we may feel well rested.

If, though, as so many of us do, we spend our days spinning plates or fighting fires or keeping all the planes and trains running smoothly and on time, and then finish work just to cook dinner or clean the house or take care of kids or spouses or pets or all of the above, we need more recovery time—and more (high-quality) sleep.

If we spend our days in loud or crowded places or other environments where we're easily and constantly overstimulated or overwhelmed, we need more sleep.

And because our brains are always on and our nervous systems so often on high alert, it can be a lot harder for us to get the sleep we so badly need. We might have trouble falling asleep. We might wake up in the middle of the night and not be able to go back to sleep. We might need either absolute silence or certain steady sounds to be able to sleep. We might wake up at the tiniest sound or movement.

Some things to try if you're highly sensitive and need more, or higher-quality, sleep:

If possible, use lower-temperature light bulbs in the evening. Red, orange, and yellow are best; avoid blue light, which can disrupt sleep cycles.

Turn off, or put down, all electronics at least an hour or two before you plan to go to bed. Many of us are sensitive to the energy from these devices, as well as the blue light. There are apps that filter out blue light, but even with those, the stimulation and bright screens won't help you sleep. I keep my phone on the other side of my bedroom and use a simple analog alarm clock when I need one.

Get blackout curtains or shades. Our circadian rhythm responds to light; darkness helps us produce melatonin, which cues the body's sleep cycle. Make sure your bedroom is dark enough.

Aromatherapy can help. Lavender and chamomile are two calming scents; research others and experiment with them to see which you prefer.

If you're sensitive to sound, a sound machine or app could be an excellent investment. The machines come in a range of sizes and prices with a variety of sound types, from pink noise (which a growing field of research suggests may be the best for sleep[2]) to white, brown, and green noise. Audiologist Amy Sarow writes, in a blog post for a hearing aid company, "While research is still growing when it comes to colored noise, brown may help with concentration, pink helps with sleep, green helps with calming, and white noise is especially good at drowning out noise from neighbors."[3]

Cut down on foods that are spicy, highly processed, high in sugar or high on the glycemic index. Studies have shown that these (at any time of day) can cause insomnia.[4,5] And as I mentioned in the section on boundaries, drinking any alcohol or eating *anything* within hours of going to bed keeps me from sleeping. I also stopped drinking caffeine many years ago—it didn't agree with my nervous system at all.

Keep a small notebook or pad and pen by the bed. When I'm lying there, tired and frustrated that I can't fall asleep, it's often because my thoughts are running at full speed, going over all I have to do tomorrow or replaying something that didn't go the way I'd hoped, or even just my grocery list. Writing it down clears out the chaos and lets my mind rest.

Do the "cognitive shuffle," a sleep hack that's gone viral on TikTok. Created by cognitive scientist and professor Luc P. Beaudoin, PhD, as a cognitive psychology student with insomnia in 1989, the technique hasn't been studied extensively but shows promise.[6] Cognitive shuffling is "imagining diverse items, scenes or processes one at a time, each for a short period of time," says Beaudoin, the creator of mySleepButton, a free app that guides users through the process.[7]

Try yoga nidra, an ancient meditation practice involving scanning the body and releasing tension and stress part by part. A quick online search will yield millions of guided meditations and instructions.

Eat when you need to

When I was younger, I was unfailingly amazed by people I knew who could skip meals with apparently no negative effects. They were busy, so they just kept doing whatever they were doing, without noticing the time or, seemingly, their bodies' signals.

My body wouldn't have it. It was very clear about when it wanted sustenance; *hangry* is a real thing.

Age and related hormonal changes seem to have significantly dimmed the *hanger* (I don't think this is a word in the "hangry" sense, but it should be!); now I sometimes have to remind myself to eat so I don't get hungry at 9 or 10 or 11 p.m.

Just because I'm not feeling hungry, though, or it's easier to work right through it and then forget I was vaguely hungry a couple of hours ago, doesn't mean I don't have to eat. Our brains and bodies need fuel, just like they need rest.

Some people who are wired differently struggle with interoception—the sense (like vision, hearing, taste, smell, and touch) that helps us feel and understand what's going on in our bodies—which can make it hard to know when we're hungry or thirsty. If you don't have this challenge, practice listening to what your body's telling you. It will let you know what it needs when it needs it.

Get outside

I almost felt silly including this. It seems so obvious (like sleep and eating well). If you've grown up here on Earth, you're very familiar by now with the benefits of fresh air and exercise and getting your daily dose of vitamin D from the sun.

But we forget. Well, *I* forget. Not like I forget where I put my car keys—when I'm hyper-focused on something for hours, or I have deadlines and am feeling stressed, I forget to make time to go outside. I forget, temporarily, how much better I feel after I've taken a long walk by the ocean. When I'm in natural light instead of artificial. When there's an actual sea breeze instead of an overhead fan.

I also forget how getting out and taking a walk when I'm stuck on something can clear my head and spark new ideas or shift my perspective and focus for a while.

I try not to schedule back-to-back meetings these days, but occasionally it's unavoidable. After a few hours of Zoom calls taken sitting at my desk in my home office, my body tells me that I need to take a break and a walk. But often, I have to be intentional about getting outside on workdays. I need to remind myself to give myself the time.

Practice calendar care

I've always had some kind of planner or system to keep me organized. When I was in grade school, it was an original Trapper Keeper (remember those? They're back!). In the '90s, my trusty Filofax was always with me. Today, I couldn't manage without Google Calendar.

Pick your app or tool—digital or analog, it doesn't matter, as long as it works for you. By which I mean that you always have access to it and you check it regularly.

I put everything on my calendar. I schedule in lunch breaks and errands. Phone calls? On the calendar. Regular meetings and one-offs, special events, travel, classes, exercise, medical appointments, and travel to and from those appointments. All on the calendar.

I also give myself some grace. Just because something's on the calendar doesn't mean it's carved in stone. There are, of course, lots of things I can't change on a whim—commitments I've made to other people or classes or group events on a set schedule. But if I've scheduled something for myself and I'm not feeling up to it or something else feels more urgent or important in the moment, I'm a responsible adult; I can change it. If I need to make a change to a meeting I have with someone else, I try hard to give more than 24 (or even 48) hours' notice; emergencies happen, but being considerate and respectful of others' time and busy schedules is important to me.

My calendar is color coded (yes, I'm one of *those* people). Not only do the colors make it easy to tell at a glance how many work meetings, social activities, and other things I have going on in a particular day or a week—and when I have a call with a friend to break up the work meetings—but they also add an element of joy to something that might otherwise be anything from bland to overwhelming. It's a small dose of color therapy that's a regular part of my workday.

I block out buffer time between meetings and before and after more time- or energy-intensive sessions or activities. It might be just 10 or 15 minutes to get more water or take a bathroom break, or half an hour or more for a walk or a meal. This creates a feeling of spaciousness and makes the inevitable context-switching less abrupt.

It's not just the feeling of spaciousness: Research shows that our brains need breaks to rest, refuel, and integrate what they're processing.[8] And a study by Bianca Acevedo, PhD, and colleagues found that "more sensitive individuals showed stronger resting-state brain connectivity indicative of greater memory and higher-order deliberative processing."[9] Sensitivityresearch.com summarizes the above research: "[T]he highly sensitive brain at rest is actually deep at work, helping individuals to integrate information, so they can remember it and be well equipped to navigate the intricacies of their environments. So, lighten up and take a break. You'll be surprised how, when you retreat into your inner world and a restful state, things start to flow."[10]

I know it's not always possible to take breaks between meetings or add buffer time to your calendar, especially in corporate settings. That makes it even more important to schedule in the critical things like lunch breaks, picking up the kids, or a class you can't miss, and also to set your starting and ending work hours in the calendar settings so colleagues can see when you're not available.

If you use a scheduling app like Calendly, take advantage of all the settings: buffer time, maximum number of meetings per day, whether someone can schedule a meeting the same day or not, etc.

Take a sound bath

Sound healing dates back at least 40,000 years to the Aborigines of Australia, and was used in ancient Greece, Egypt, Nepal, Tibet and India, among other cultures. Although music and sound therapy have been shown to help release tension and anxiety, improve blood flow, reduce muscle stiffness, improve sleep, and relieve many different types of pain, scientific explanations are still mostly theoretical.

The instruments used in a sound bath might include crystal singing bowls, gongs, bells, cymbals, drums, didgeridoos, tuning forks, and chimes. They all vibrate at various frequencies that are thought to affect us in different ways, by acting tactilely on the body and through entrainment, which helps sync our brain waves to the more relaxed alpha and theta states.[11,12]

There are endless modalities that help reduce stress and promote rest. I'm singling out sound healing because it's less well known and more easily accessible than many. Where I live, hours from any major metro area, I was surprised to find several practitioners with affordable offerings in a range of venues, and I've tried a few.

I had a very different experience at each sound bath. The first, at a yoga studio, was more noise than sound healing to my sensitive ears and nervous system; the newish practitioner clearly enjoyed experimenting with startling sounds. The second was more soothing sound-wise, hosted in a private home by a practitioner with many years' experience, but we were crammed close together in a small space, which I found a little uncomfortable. The third was hosted by a woman who facilitates sound baths in different environments, including chapels and large swimming pools where you can lie in a "floatie" and absorb the sound over the water. I attended one held at a retreat center in a large open room; it was calming and restorative. I'll definitely be going to more of her offerings.

Protect your energy

If you're an empath, someone who easily and unintentionally picks up other people's emotions and/or physical sensations, you need a way to protect your own energy and keep other influences out.

I promised I'd share the technique the psychic Victoria Bullis taught me to create a bubble around myself—an impermeable membrane that only allows what I want to pass through.

Before you go out, while you're in a safe place in a comfortable position, close your eyes or soft-focus on something that won't distract you.

- ❖ Imagine a bubble that surrounds you completely.
- ❖ Decide how thick the membrane is, and how far away from your body—an inch all the way around? A foot?
- ❖ Picture what it's made of, and what it looks like. What color is it? Is it completely transparent? Translucent? Is

the surface matte or shiny? Does it have a texture or any features like sparkles or a shimmer?

- ✤ Set an intention for what it will let in and out. For example, you might want to let only positive or beneficial energy in and only negative energy out.
- ✤ Play with it a bit. Imagine extending it out a few more inches or feet, to create a larger protective space around you. Then draw it in, closer to your body. See if you can sense the difference.
- ✤ You can also play with the color, translucence, material, and texture of your bubble. See what feels right.

This gets easier with practice. I use it sometimes in airports or crowded places where I want a little more personal space. Try it. Notice how people around you respond. They won't be able to see it, but they may well sense it.

Find your micro-moments of joy

Designer and author Ingrid Fetell Lee has spent a lot of time researching joy. A professor's comment during her first year-end review in design school, that her work gave him a feeling of joy, put her on a path that sparked a TED talk, a book called *Joyful: The Surprising Power of Ordinary Things to Create Extraordinary Happiness* (Little, Brown Spark, 2018), and a blog, *The Aesthetics of Joy*. I recommend all three.

In one blog post, "Hidden signs you're headed for burnout—and how to stop it,"[13] Lee talks about planning micro-moments of joy. She breaks them out into categories:

"*Lifesavers* are quick, active joy breaks you can take to help relieve pressure when you're under a lot of stress. Research shows that small moments of joy can relieve the cardiovascular effects of stress on the body—lowering cortisol, heart rate, and blood pressure. Think of them like a reset button for your day."

Examples of lifesavers might include dancing to your favorite song, watching a few minutes of a comedian you love, playing with a pet or child, or taking a quick walk or run in nature.

"*Mini-vacations* are restorative activities that help recharge your batteries." They're "play for adults," which, as Lee defines them, "can last anywhere from 10 minutes to a full day."

Examples of a mini-vacation might be working on an art or craft project, or a jigsaw puzzle; going to a park, going for a swim, or playing a game of tennis or frisbee; exploring a different neighborhood or nearby town; spending a lazy morning or evening in when you'd usually go out.

"*Hip hip hoorays* are ways of celebrating little bits of good news in the everyday," and can be done alone or with loved ones.

Examples of hip hip hoorays could be a special meal or treat, a happy selfie taken the moment you learn about good news, a small gift or decoration left on someone's desk or bed, or singing or dancing together.

What I love about the concept is that you don't have to strategize or plan much. For lifesavers, all you need is a little self-awareness and creativity. What brings you joy? Smelling flowers in a seasonal garden? Bird watching? Taking photos? Coloring? Walking barefoot on the grass or sand? Reading a few pages of a novel? These all take only a few minutes and can make a world of difference in your day. The min-vacation ideas and hip hip hoorays don't have to take much longer or cost any money. They're accessible to all of us.

Ask for what you want and what you need

Just as I was uncomfortable being taken care of during my Mexican resort stay, many of us are uncomfortable asking for what we want or need when it's anything more complicated than ordering a drink at the swim-up bar.

Beyond the obvious, though—that we'll never get what we want if we don't ask for it—there are other reasons to learn to do this.

Clarity is kindness. Being clear ourselves about what we want or need, and expressing it clearly, reduces confusion and makes things easier for the people around us. As much as we might wish our loved ones could read our minds, they usually can't (and we can't usually read theirs either). And I don't know about you, but I wouldn't have wanted any of my colleagues or bosses inside my head—so it's only right that we're clear and direct with them.

(Most) people get joy from helping others. You know that little dopamine hit you get from giving someone a gift? Why deprive others of the satisfaction of doing something for you? We get those chemical highs from both giving and receiving, so letting others give you something you want is its own virtuous cycle. Everyone wins.

Make your own life easier. In late 2023, I was adopted by a handsome senior cat named Zephyr. Zephyr appeared at my door the day I moved into the condo I was renting. I gradually learned his story: He'd been adopted, with his sister, Iris, by a local family

17 years ago. They moved several times, and Zephyr, who was a highly sensitive cat, was upset by all the moves and started spraying inside the house. The family put him out. They continued to leave him food and water outside, but wouldn't let him inside anymore. So Zephyr, who was also a very smart cat, made friends with a lot of neighborhood humans, including a man who lived across the street from my place. The man fed Zephyr, took care of him and loved him for a few years. The cat came and went, and they were both content.

Until the man moved to Los Angeles. He thought about taking Zephyr with him, but didn't know how the older cat would do on the long drive or in the new place, and assumed he had a family that would take care of him here. I later learned that the day Zephyr came to greet me was the day after my neighbor moved to LA. A *very* smart cat.

Anyway, despite the facts that I'm allergic to cats, there was no room for a litter box in my little place, and my lease forbid me from having a pet, Zephyr quickly worked his way into my heart and my apartment.

Zephyr was a chatty cat with a lot of different meows. As he and I are both good at reading a room and sensing energies, we often understood each other. Then again, there were plenty of times we didn't. I tried to explain to him why he had to get into the borrowed cat carrier when I wanted the vet to check him out. I tried to explain why I needed to trim his claws.

Alas, he spoke no English, and more to the point, I spoke no cat. I understood his "I'm hungry" and "I'm thirsty" meows. I got it when he wanted to get into a room with a closed door or go outside. I learned when he wanted to be picked up, and it was very clear when he wanted to be put down.

But there were meows that I just couldn't understand, no matter how hard both of us tried. If only Zephyr had been able to tell me clearly what he wanted, life would've been easier for both of us. Although it may sometimes feel like we're speaking a different language than our boss, colleagues, partner, or kids, the good news is that when we're dealing with other humans, we can all get better at asking for what we need.

Find your community

I'll never forget a conversation, the week before college graduation, with a classmate who came into my dorm room to chat. We were talking about post-commencement plans: He was going to grad school in New England, where he was from. I'd deferred my grad school for a year to go to New Zealand—I'd gotten a work permit through a study-abroad program that was open to new graduates.

"You're so lucky," he said. "I've never even left New England."

At the time, my first thought was that luck had nothing to do with it. I'd worked for what I had. I decided I wanted something and went after it. He, on the other hand, came from a wealthy family; he had privilege I couldn't even imagine.

Looking back, two things strike me. One is that he was right: I was very fortunate. I may not have come from money, but I did come from a family that had traveled extensively, had lived abroad, spoke multiple languages. I was exposed to all of this from birth and grew up being curious about other cultures and other parts of the world. My classmate could easily have asked his parents for a plane ticket to New Zealand and gotten it (first class!), but it wouldn't have occurred to him.

The second is that he also was lucky, and not just in the sense of coming from wealth. He lived in the house he was born in, surrounded by the same friends and family. He had a solid foundation—a community—that I, with my peripatetic childhood and social awkwardness, had never had.

My peripatetic adulthood didn't help. I have no regrets about all the traveling and living abroad I've done and hope to continue to do; it's made me who I am and given me countless incredible experiences and friends I never would've met otherwise. But those friends are scattered around the world; I can't just text them and see if anyone wants to grab lunch or go for a walk. I'm really missing community.

Community's a theme that came up in many of the interviews and conversations I had for and about this book. As highly perceptive people who are wired a little differently, we do often feel alone or misunderstood. And finding our tribe, people we can relate to more easily, can make a world of difference. It's why I created my mastermind, the G.R.I.T. Collaborative, with small-group cohorts of highly perceptive women leaders. In each small group, we cocreate a safe space that can be very hard to find in other parts of our lives—especially for those who feel they have to mask in their work environments. And we share questions, challenges, successes, and experiences, and learn together. (G.R.I.T.'s an acronym for *grace, resilience, intuition,* and *trust,* the four pillars of the program.)

Tricia Livermore, the heart-centered coach, talked about the importance of finding a supportive community in a professional context: "Find people who will have your back. Mentors, coaches, peers who can support you, whether emotionally, in the role, or collectively; it doesn't matter. Just make sure that you've got trusted people you can lean on. It's like having your own personal advisory board. I didn't always understand the value of that, and I didn't have it. Now I know how important it is to create your community of support. It isn't always easy to find inside the company you work for and might require some effort to find outside. The more you put it out there that you're looking for a particular kind of group or people, the more easily you'll find it or them."

I'll end this chapter with Kalen Cobb emphasizing the need for both community and self-care in healing from—and preventing a relapse into—burnout: "I think there's also a level of burnout that continues to exist within you, almost like a scar," Kalen noted. "You can get the skills to cope, you can get the community, and you will continue living life; you will continue making joy and beauty. But there is a level of burnout that at the cellular, soul level, you will always remember. It's a reminder for me that I don't want to go back to that space. Tending to myself, caring for myself, being with friends, being with community, is important to make sure that if I see I'm starting to go into that spiral, I know how to get out of it."

Whether or not we've experienced burnout (and I'm not sure I've met any highly perceptive woman leader who hasn't), it's always a risk, especially for those of us who feel deeply and think differently. Kalen's comments are a beautiful reminder: We need to take better care of ourselves both to heal from what we've gone through and to prevent it from happening again. And we have to listen to our bodies and souls to figure out what that means for us.

Takeaways

- ☑ Self-care doesn't have to cost a lot of money—or even any at all. It also doesn't have to take a lot of time. But the costs of not taking care of yourself can be very high.
- ☑ Simple things, like getting enough sleep, fresh air, healthy food, and breaks to rest and refuel your brain, set the foundation.
- ☑ Make time for things that bring you joy—every micro-moment counts.
- ☑ Ask for what you want, and ask for help when you need it.
- ☑ Find your community. As strong and competent as so many of us are, we can't go it alone.

Conclusion

One of my goals in writing this book was to introduce you to a range of women leaders from very different backgrounds who all identify as having certain sensitivities, and to share their stories along with my own. Each of these women is highly perceptive and has experienced both the challenges and the gifts that come with the trait. In a couple of cases, the interviewees didn't self-identify as highly sensitive but found that many of the traits that are common to HSPs—the ones I describe in this book—resonated strongly with them.

I've been asked by a lot of high-sensory women for case studies of leaders who've succeeded despite their sensitivity or different wiring. A few people have also asked for stories of those who haven't done as well—cautionary tales, I guess, of what not to do, or how not to handle oneself in the workplace. I've tried to provide a balanced perspective: no trait is 100 percent positive or negative, and without one side, we wouldn't recognize or appreciate the other. That said, so many of us, including most of the women you've met here, grew up with messages—subtle or very strong—

that the way we naturally were was somehow wrong and needed to be fixed or changed. So I've tried to emphasize the gifts, as well as how we can support ourselves in managing the challenges.

And since I wanted to end on a high note, I was excited to happen across Mindy Yang, and thrilled when she agreed to talk with me for *Perceptive*. The bio on her website says, "Mindy is a multifaceted strategist renowned for her expertise in sensory experiences, entrepreneurship, and immersive, human-centric brand, product, and experience design. As a distinguished sensory expert, flavor hacker, olfactory artist, and scent creator, she excels in crafting innovative and evocative experiences that engage the senses and captivate audiences."[1]

Mindy's always been, in her words, "sensually sensitive, a super-taster and super-smeller." Sensitive to energies and emotions, too, and with a tendency to "carry other people's burdens," Mindy found living in New York City during the pandemic too much, so she and her husband bought a farm and moved to the Hudson Valley. And she told me she's never been so happy.

She's also always been interested in why people do what they do. Mindy studied psychology and worked in a neuropsychology lab as an undergrad and became a Reiki master in her 20s. A naturally curious, open and intuitive person, she learned other holistic healing techniques as well, to keep herself grounded.

I'm intrigued by the way Mindy's multipotentialite interests and career paths started and became intertwined. Early on she worked in brand experience design, typically a primarily visual field. That led to immersive experience design for events, which involved not only the aesthetics but also the ambient sound or music, the catering menu, and so on. She described working with restaurant brands on signage, menus and more, and "playing with my superpower of synesthesia and being able to understand intuitively when people need red versus something that's pastel, and it's the blue and yellow."

She shared some things she's learned along the way that have helped her consulting clients sell more of their products or services: "Did you know that if something is round in shape, [people tend to perceive it as] more buttery, luscious, and sweeter, versus something that is square, rectangular, or triangular? Those tend to be perceived as saltier, spicier, and/or crunchier, even though they're exactly the same thing. In engineering future snacks, in playing with how people perceive a hospitality experience, these things really come into play. Also, if you play really loud rock music at a small bar, same exact paint and furnishing, but if it's loud music, people drink more alcohol and they eat less. In certain white tablecloth settings, without ambiance but with classical music playing in the background, people will pay more for the same exact meal."

Mindy told me, "I try to use these sensory powers for good, and also educate people. These nuances matter, and I also want to balance the scale. To help people understand all the little marketing levelers at work, so they can be discerning customers, because it's kind of not fair." Using our "sensory powers for good" is one of my favorite phrases from a fascinating conversation.

In our short meeting, there wasn't time to touch on all of Mindy's various ventures or her experience crafting bespoke fragrances and flavors, creating Perfumarie, a "beauty and wellness incubator," running an organic farm, offering functional wellness products made from herbs and other ingredients grown on her farm, or many other companies and initiatives she's founded or cofounded. We did talk about the nonprofit World Taste & Smell Association, of which she's the chief engagement officer and cofounder, and an incredible-sounding event that was planned for the week following our interview: the Global Taste & Smell Summit in New York City. One of the highlights of the summit that Mindy mentioned specifically was a "cross-modal mindfulness brunch," to include a sound bath and discussion of "sonic seasoning" and end with a cacao ceremony. I couldn't make it to New York for the event but am hoping it was so successful that we'll be learning about Global Taste & Smell Summits in other locations sometime soon.

I don't think I've ever met someone who's doing so much at once (she also hosts a podcast and blogs prolifically). I asked Mindy about this, and she explained that many of her efforts support each other: "I think it's the Japanese word 'ikigai.' I think I found it. They balance each other." (*Ikigai* is the Japanese concept that your reason for being can be found at the intersection of four areas: what you love, what you're good at, what you can be paid for, and what the world needs.)

She continued with an example of an upcoming trip she, her husband, and her mother-in-law are taking together: "It's a little bit self-serving in the sense that everything is easy. I work all the time. But I'm going on holiday with my husband, and his mother really wants to see the aurora. So we're going back to Iceland, and we're going to a Michelin-starred restaurant. I'm going to introduce myself to the sommelier so we can hang out and get special treatment, but really learn about his life. And then we can maybe make a podcast episode or write about it. It all works. My husband is in hospitality. He designs hotels and restaurants and Michelin-star-level restaurants. So everyone in my life is really into what I do."

I commented that it doesn't sound self-serving at all—it sounds like living in flow. Mindy agreed and added, "And no two days are the same, which is what I need too." I understand completely, and suspect that you might, as well.

Mindy Yang embodies what I support my clients in doing: (re)designing and (re)aligning life and work to create the conditions they need to thrive. It's not always easy, as Mindy says it is for her now, but it *is* possible, and although we didn't talk about it in these terms, I suspect that at least a few of the other women leaders you've met here live in flow at least some of the time.

I asked Mindy what advice she had for highly perceptive women in particular who might not yet know what some of their superpowers are or might be struggling with some of the challenges that come with being highly sensitive. Her response: "Be incredibly kind to yourself. Just be incredibly kind. I take this advice all the time. Every second is a moment to reset. Start again when you're ready, but find time if you need to recharge, recover. I use the word selfish in a cheeky way, but saying no is awesome. Learn to say no and find people that want what you want, because that energy, in my opinion, speaking as a Reiki master, amplifies. That's the catalyst."

She talked about the fact that except for two scientists, no one working for her nonprofit gets paid, including Mindy herself. She hopes that will change for all of them, but "at this time it's an honor and a pleasure because the people in my tribe are just incredible."

She added, "Most people are like, 'It's crazy. It's never gonna happen, can't be done.' Well, it *can* be done. And remaining optimistic—it's important. The second you take on a victim position and spiral into depression, you're wasting your energy. And that energy is too precious. Use it to hug yourself in and recover. We're doing things."

What do you want your life to look like?

I admit that I'm still working on bringing more flow into my own life. I have the vision; I've made some major changes and started creating it. Some pieces are falling into place more quickly and easily than others. But I'm slowly, surely, building the life I want for myself.

In the section on boundaries in Chapter 3, I mentioned a visioning exercise I often do with clients. You can do this yourself if your picture of the future isn't as clear as you'd like it to be. Here's one version—you may want to record yourself reading the instructions out loud so you can play it back for yourself as a guided visualization.

- ❖ Sit comfortably, with your feet resting on the floor. Relax your shoulders. Close your eyes or, if you'd prefer, soft-focus on a blank wall, a candle flame, or another object in your room that won't distract you.
- ❖ Take a few deep, calming breaths. Try to exhale for a few counts longer than you inhale.
- ❖ Choose a time in the nearish future—anywhere between six months and three to five years from now usually feels manageable. This is just something to start with; it doesn't have to be forever.

- Imagine that you're gently lifted out of the current timeline and set down in your future life at the time you've decided on. You're happy in this new life you've built. You're spending your time intentionally, the way you want to, with people you love. You're where you want to be.
- With your eyes still closed or soft-focused, get a good "look" or feel around you—what do you notice?
- Note what you observe. Where are you? Is it your home? Work? Is it a place you recognize, or new to you? What does the place look like? How is it decorated? What colors surround you? Furnishings? What's the light like? If there are windows, what do you see when you look outside?
- If this place isn't your home, what is your home like? Where is it located? Who lives there with you?
- Run through all your senses. Can you hear anything? Smell anything? Do you notice any specific textures around you? What's the temperature like? How are you dressed?
- Are there people with you, or nearby? If so, who? Are they people you recognize, or are they new to you? What's your relationship with them?
- How do you spend your time now? What do your mornings look like? Your afternoons? Evenings? What kind of work are you doing, if any? Do you follow a similar routine most days, or is every day different? Do you work alone or with others? What do you do for fun? To relax? For exercise? What are mealtimes like?

- ♣ Who do you love spending time with in this new life, and what brings you joy? How much time do you spend with these people and doing these things?
- ♣ Take a few minutes in silence to observe and absorb. Notice how you feel in this life you've built for yourself, surrounded by people and things you love. Where in your body do the feelings sit? Notice anything else that comes up for you.
- ♣ Take a snapshot in your mind, an image to help you remember what you envisioned later, when you're back in your current life.
- ♣ When you're ready, take a few more calming breaths, and slowly come back to today, your chair, and the room you're in.

You may want to take a few minutes to write down any thoughts that come up—what you saw and felt, any details of the experience that you don't want to forget. Then, ask yourself a few questions:

- o What was different about that future life? How were you different?
- o How do you feel about the major differences between that life and your current one?
- o What are some changes you'd need to make to start creating the life you envisioned?
- o How do you feel about those changes?
- o What's one small step you can take now to get started on that path?

- When will you commit to taking it?
- What kind of support do you need for the journey?

Giving ourselves grace

In the Introduction, I wrote that I have a lot of empathy and compassion for the person I was when I burned myself out so severely that I had to leave my old life behind and start again (in Peru!). If I'd had a book like this one back then, with stories from others like me, not only would I not have felt so alone—I would have made some very different choices earlier on. I like to think I wouldn't have reached burnout, or at least would've realized it sooner and made some big changes before it got as bad as it did.

If I'd known then what I do now, I wouldn't have worked my ass off so consistently for so many years, especially in jobs I didn't even enjoy.

I would've focused a lot more on finding my community.

I would've let go of some of the things I held onto for way too long.

I would've had more fun! And intentionally found ways to bring more joy into my life.

I would've been easier on myself and given myself some grace.

I'm not all the way there yet; I still have plenty of work to do myself. It's a journey! But I'm clear on my own values, goals, and boundaries in a way I'd never stopped to think about years ago. I make decisions that are aligned with them. If I fail, I take what I can learn from it and move on. And when I succeed, I celebrate those wins. I've also gotten better at asking for help. It's still not easy, but I know now that none of us can go it alone.

If you identify as perceptive, highly sensitive, neurodivergent, or simply wired a little differently, I hope that reading the stories of others with similar traits brings fresh perspective, and that the tips and tools on self-care and throughout the rest of the book are helpful in managing the challenges that come with your gifts. And maybe even in accepting your gifts. We all have a superpower or two (or more). Embracing them doesn't mean denying that we sometimes struggle—it's not either/or. They're two sides of the same coin.

Most importantly, I hope you now have a better sense of how much value you bring to the world, and know that you're not crazy, you're not broken, and you're not alone.

Reflection questions

For individuals:

- Of all the strengths and superpowers discussed in *Perceptive*—deep empathy, the ability to read a room, the ability to connect the dots, see several steps ahead, or see both the big picture and the details, conscientiousness, a need for authenticity, strong commitment to social justice, and more—which resonate with you? Which do you claim?
- Have you always known that these are gifts that not everyone has? How has the book changed the way you think about them or yourself?
- What about the challenges covered in the book—people pleasing, lack of boundaries, frustration with seeing what others don't? Which do you identify with?
- Has reading *Perceptive* helped you reframe any of them, or consider new ways to manage or effectively overcome them? In what ways?

- When have you ignored your intuition or your heart and made a decision you later regretted? What might be helpful for you the next time you have a "head vs. heart" decision to make?
- What changes can you make to your working environment and conditions that would support you and help you flourish? What about at home?
- Are you a perfectionist? If so, what might change if you were able to let go of some of the details, the need for control? What would be helpful for you in starting to let go?
- If you manage people, how comfortable are you with delegating? Do you encourage others to work within their zones of genius so you can thrive in yours?
- How do you feel about receiving feedback? About giving it? Does anything the leaders shared change your perspective on either one?
- What's your experience with burnout? If you've been there before, do you think you'll recognize the signs before it happens again? What would it take for you to make any changes you need to prevent it from happening again?
- What ideas or inspiration can you take from the chapter on self-care and implement for yourself?

For team and organizational leaders and HR/People/ DEI professionals:

- How does knowing that up to 30 percent of your team or organization has many of the strengths and challenges described in this book affect the way you think about your team or workplace culture?

- What changes could you make that would benefit not only the highly perceptive and the neurodivergent employees in your organization, but all employees? Consider changes to policies and procedures, the way decisions about hiring and promotions are made, the way meetings are scheduled and run, and how information is communicated throughout the company.

- Did anything in *Perceptive* change your thinking about behaviors you might have noticed or questioned in specific individuals? The goal is not to call anyone out or excuse bad behavior. It's to open up to new potential explanations for something that's unexpected or different from the "typical"—and create opportunities and conditions for those who are wired a little differently to shine. When all employees (and leaders) in the organization are thriving, everyone benefits.

Endnotes

Chapter 1

1. "About Sensitivity," Sensitivityresearch.com, accessed October 2024, https://sensitivityresearch.com/about-sensitivity/.
2. Elaine N Aron, PhD, *The Highly Sensitive Person: How to Thrive When the World Overwhelms You* (Citadel Press, 2013), 5.
3. Clare Kumar, host, Happy Space Podcast, episode 5, "There are No Ambiverts—with Jenn Turnham," May 2, 2022, 45 min,. 26 sec., https://clarekumar.com/podcast/ep_5-there-are-no-ambiverts/.
4. David DiSalvo, "Your Brain Sees Even When You Don't," *Forbes*, June 22, 2013, https://www.forbes.com/sites/daviddisalvo/2013/06/22/your-brain-sees-even-when-you-dont/.
5. Dr. Esther Bergsma, "The HSP Brain," October 18, 2023, 24 min., 42 sec., https://www.youtube.com/watch?v=Yg5-911-h5c.
6. Katherine Maslowski, "Hormones and pain: How your cycle affects sensitivity," Hormona, August 1, 2023, https://www.hormona.io/blog/hormones-and-pain-during-cycle/.

7. Corrie Pelc, "How sleep loss may lead to heightened pain sensitivity," *Medical News Today*, October 31, 2023, https://www.medicalnewstoday.com/articles/how-sleep-loss-may-lead-to-heightened-pain-sensitivity.
8. Sensitivityresearch.com, "About Sensitivity."
9. Sensitivityresearch.com, "About Sensitivity."
10. Bianca P. Acevedo, Elaine N. Aron, Arthur Aron, Tracy Cooper, and Robert Marhenke, "Sensory processing sensitivity and its relation to sensation seeking," *Current Research in Behavioral Sciences*, volume 4 (2023): 100100, https://doi.org/10.1016/j.crbeha.2023.100100.
11. Acevedo et al, "Sensory processing sensitivity and its relation to sensation seeking," 100100.
12. Anita Moorjani, *Sensitive is the New Strong: The Power of Empaths in an Increasingly Harsh World*, (Atria/Enliven Books, 2021), 1.
13. Judith Orloff, MD, "Are You a Physical Empath?" *Psychology Today*, February 8, 2014, https://www.psychologytoday.com/us/blog/the-genius-of-empathy/201402/are-you-a-physical-empath.

Chapter 2

1. Sara Luterman and Kate Sosin, "Who coined the term 'neurodiversity?' It wasn't Judy Singer, some autistic advocates say," The 19th, April 23, 2024, https://19thnews.org/2024/04/neurodiversity-term-judy-singer-autistic-advocates/.
2. Ed Thompson, "Why Neurodiversity is Misunderstood in the Workplace," *Psychology Today*, June 13, 2024, https://www.psychologytoday.com/us/blog/a-hidden-force/202406/why-neurodiversity-is-misunderstood-in-the-workplace.

3. Nick Walker, PhD, "Neurodiversity: Some Basic Terms & Definitions," Neuroqueer: The Writings of Dr. Nick Walker, accessed November 2024, https://neuroqueer.com/neurodiversity-terms-and-definitions/.
4. Szabolcs David, Lucy L. Brown, Anneriet M. Heemskerk, Elaine Aron, et al. "Sensory processing sensitivity and axonal microarchitecture: Identifying brain structural characteristics for behavior," *Brain Structure & Function*, 227 (2022), 2769–2785, https://doi.org/10.1007/s00429-022-02571-1.
5. Bianca Acevedo, PhD, "What is Sensory Processing Sensitivity? Traits, Insights, and ADHD Links," *ADDitude*, updated February 14, 2025, https://www.additudemag.com/highly-sensitive-person-sensory-processing-sensitivity-adhd/.
6. Luchuan Xiao, Kris Baetens, and Natacha Deroost, "Unraveling the highly sensitive mind: an explorative study of the cognitive mechanism underlying sensory processing sensitivity," Brussels University Consultation Center, May 9, 2022, https://researchportal.vub.be/en/publications/unraveling-the-highly-sensitive-mind-an-explorative-study-of-the-.
7. David Bridges and Haline E. Schendan, "Sensitive individuals are more creative," *Personality and Individual Differences*, vol. 142 (2019): 186-195, https://colab.ws/articles/10.1016%2Fj.paid.2018.09.015.
8. Emma Craddock, "'You Don't Look Autistic': Why Neurodivergent Women Have Been Sidelined," *The Wire*, February 29, 2024, https://thewire.in/health/neurodivergent-women-sidelined-audhd.
9. "Advocating for Other Undiagnosed Autistic Women," MelanieDeziel.com, accessed November 2024, https://www.melaniedeziel.com/advocacy.

10. Bianca Acevedo, Elaine Aron, Sarah Pospos and Dana Jessen, "The functional highly sensitive brain: a review of the brain circuits underlying sensory processing sensitivity and seemingly related disorders," *Philosophical Transactions of the Royal Society B,* vol. 373, issue 1744 (*2018*), https://royalsocietypublishing.org/doi/10.1098/rstb.2017.0161.
11. "Free Autism Quiz for the Sensitive," JulieBjelland.com, accessed February 5, 2025, https://www.juliebjelland.com/autism-quiz.

Chapter 3

1. Heather Thompson, host, *Recipes for Success,* season 5, episode 2, "Rachel Radway on Boundaries," July 18, 2024, 46 min., 8 sec., https://open.spotify.com/episode/1t8Y1GlRBpLzmAFxEsyyAb?si=6e547c734f1e4c25.

Chapter 4

1. Esther Bergsma, *The Brain of the Highly Sensitive Person: Why you shouldn't judge a fish by its ability to climb a tree* (Booklight Publishing, 2020), 26.
2. Bergsma, *The Brain of the Highly Sensitive Person,* 26.
3. Thomas R. Verny, MD, "Intuition: What It Is and How It Works," *Psychology Today,* updated August 22, 2023, https://www.psychologytoday.com/us/blog/explorations-of-the-mind/202308/intuition-what-it-is-and-how-it-works.
4. Verny, "Intuition."

Chapter 5

1. Bergsma, *The Brain of the Highly Sensitive Person,* 91–101.
2. Bergsma, *The Brain of the Highly Sensitive Person,* 94.

3. "Identify and unleash your talent," BCS, The Chartered Institute for IT, July 24, 2019, https://www.bcs.org/articles-opinion-and-research/identify-and-unleash-your-talent/.
4. Ludmila N. Praslova, *The Canary Code: A Guide to Neurodiversity, Dignity, and Intersectional Belonging at Work* (Berrett-Koehler Publishers, 2024), 3.
5. Donald Sull, Charles Sull, and Ben Zweig, "Toxic Culture is Driving the Great Resignation," *MIT Sloan Management Review*, January 11, 2022, https://sloanreview.mit.edu/article/toxic-culture-is-driving-the-great-resignation/.
6. Donald Sull, Charles Sull, William Cipolli, and Caio Brighenti, "Why Every Leader Needs to Worry About Toxic Culture," *MIT Sloan Management Review*, March 16, 2022, https://sloanreview.mit.edu/article/why-every-leader-needs-to-worry-about-toxic-culture/.
7. Ludmila N. Praslova, "Feeling Distressed at Work? It Might Be More Than Burnout," *Fast Company*, January 14, 2022, http://www.fastcompany.com/90712671/feeling-distressed-at-work-it-might-be-more-than-burnout.
8. Praslova, "Feeling Distressed at Work."

Chapter 6

1. "Masking," *Psychology Today*, accessed November 2024, https://www.psychologytoday.com/us/basics/masking.

Chapter 7

1. "Burnout," ICD-11 for Morbidity and Mortality Statistics, accessed February 2025, https://icd.who.int/browse/2024-01/mms/en#129180281.

2. Beth Sissons, "What to know about neurodivergent burnout," *Medical News Today*, July 16, 2024, https://www.medicalnewstoday.com/articles/neurodivergent-burnout.
3. Dr. Natalie Engelbrecht, "Burnout vs. autistic burnout," Embrace Autism, updated May 27, 2024, https://embrace-autism.com/burnout-vs-autistic-burnout/.
4. Sissons, "What to know about neurodivergent burnout."
5. "The unique experience of neurodivergent burnout," Creased Puddle blog, September 25, 2023, https://www.creasedpuddle.co.uk/the-unique-experience-of-neurodivergent-burnout/.
6. Sissons, "What to know about neurodivergent burnout."

Chapter 8

1. Jenn Granneman, "14 Things Highly Sensitive People Need for Happiness," *Psychology Today*, August 10, 2018, https://www.psychologytoday.com/us/blog/the-secret-lives-introverts/201808/14-things-highly-sensitive-people-need-happiness.
2. Carla K. Johnson, "Have you tried pink noise for sleep? Here's what to know," *AP News*, updated May 20, 2024, https://apnews.com/article/pink-brown-white-noise-sleep-focus-concentration-f5f24dad1effb09c1cf8b607bd22ebc7.
3. Amy Sarow, "White, Brown, Pink and Green Noise: Benefits of Each," Soundly blog, June 11, 2024, https://www.soundly.com/blog/white-noise-and-alternatives.
4. Jillian Kubala, MS, RD, "6 Foods That Keep You Awake at Night," *Healthline*, July 7, 2021, https://www.healthline.com/nutrition/foods-that-keep-you-awake.
5. "Refined Carbs May Trigger Insomnia, Finds Study," Columbia University Irving Medical Center, December 11, 2019, https://

www.cuimc.columbia.edu/news/refined-carbs-may-trigger-insomnia-finds-study.
6. Hannah Yasharoff, "How to Try the Viral 'Cognitive Shuffling' Hack for a Better Night's Sleep, According to Psychology Experts," *Women's Health*, July 26, 2024, https://www.womenshealthmag.com/health/a61580910/cognitive-shuffling/.
7. "The Cognitive Science," mySleepButton.com, accessed October 2024, https://mysleepbutton.com/en/support/the-cognitive-science/.
8. "Research Proves Your Brain Needs Breaks," Microsoft.com Work Trend Index Special Report, April 20, 2021, https://www.microsoft.com/en-us/worklab/work-trend-index/brain-research#research%2520%23wellness%2520%23productivity%2520%23microsoft.
9. Bianca P. Acevedo, Tyler Santander, Robert Marhenke, Arthur Aron, and Elaine Aron,. "Sensory Processing Sensitivity Predicts Individual Differences in Resting-State Functional Connectivity Associated with Depth of Processing," Neuropsychobiology 80 (2021):185-200, https://doi.org/10.1159/000513527.
10. Bianca P. Acevedo, "The Highly Active, Highly Sensitive Brain at Rest," Sensitivityresearch.com, August 11, 2021, https://sensitivityresearch.com/the-highly-active-highly-sensitive-brain-at-rest/.
11. Marlynn Wei, MD, JD, "The Healing Power of Sound as Meditation," *Psychology Today*, updated January 16, 2024, https://www.psychologytoday.com/us/blog/urban-survival/201907/the-healing-power-of-sound-as-meditation.

12. Vicky Foreman, "The science and history of sound therapy," SleepHub.com blog, July 26, 2021, https://www.sleephub.com/blogs/articles/the-science-and-history-of-sound-therapy.
13. Ingrid Fetell Lee, "Hidden Signs You're Headed for Burnout—and How to Stop It," The Aesthetics of Joy, accessed February 23, 2025, https://aestheticsofjoy.com/hidden-signs-youre-headed-for-burnout-and-how-to-stop-it/.

Conclusion

1. "Meet Mindy Yang," mindyyang.info, accessed February 23, 2025, https://mindyyang.info/.

Resources

There are so many books, websites, podcasts, and YouTube channels out there on the topics I've covered in *Perceptive* that I can't possibly list them all. The following are resources I myself have learned from, found helpful, and can recommend. If you've found others you like, I'd love to hear about them.

Quizzes & self-assessments

Elaine Aron and the team at sensitivityresearch.com have updated the original self-test for high sensitivity; the new version has fewer questions and allows for more nuanced responses. The test for adults (age 18 and older) is available:

- on Aron's site at https://hsperson.com/test/highly-sensitive-test/ (you'll need to print it out or write down your responses) and
- on the research site at https://sensitivityresearch.com/self-tests/adult-self-test-updated/ (interactive)

Both sites offer other tests too (all are interactive):

- *Is your child highly sensitive?* https://hsperson.com/test/highly-sensitive-child-test/
- *Are you a sensation seeker?* https://hsperson.com/test/high-sensation-seeking-test/
- Test for children to take themselves (8–18 years): https://sensitivityresearch.com/self-tests/test-for-children-8-18-years/
- Test your child (4–18 years): https://sensitivityresearch.com/self-tests/test-for-parents-and-children-8-18-years/
- Test your student (6-10 years): https://sensitivityresearch.com/self-tests/test-for-parents-and-children-8-18-years/

Julie Bjelland updates her site frequently and is currently offering one quiz for both sensitivity and autism: https://www.juliebjelland.com/autism-quiz.

Dr. Natalie Engelbrecht and the team at Embrace Autism offer several more in-depth tests for anyone who suspects they might be autistic or have ADHD. These are widely used tools that, in some cases, contain outdated questions and assumptions. Dr. Engelbrecht has rated each one on appropriate and respectful wording, clarity, and lack of ambiguity (I found myself frustrated by the lack of specificity and context on many of the questions—and if you are autistic, you can laugh with me about this on a meta level), and testing accuracy, and listed available versions (in different languages for various age groups) plus information on how to take each test and what the scores mean.

Read the descriptions and notes for each, and take them when you're feeling comfortable, open, and honest with yourself. You might find that you answer certain questions differently at different stages of your own journey of discovery.

- Autism Spectrum Quotient: https://embrace-autism.com/autism-spectrum-quotient/
- RAADS-R ("designed to identify adult autistics who 'escape diagnosis' due to a subclinical level presentation"): https://embrace-autism.com/raads-r/
- Adult ADHD Self-Report Scale: https://embrace-autism.com/asrs-5/
- Camouflaging Autistic Traits Questionnaire: https://embrace-autism.com/cat-q/
- Aspie Quiz: https://embrace-autism.com/aspie-quiz/

Books

Aron, Elaine N, PhD. *The Highly Sensitive Person: How to Thrive When the World Overwhelms You.* Citadel Press, 2013.

Bergsma, Esther. *The Brain of the Highly Sensitive Person: Why you shouldn't judge a fish by its ability to climb a tree.* Booklight Publishing, 2020.

Fetell Lee, Ingrid. *Joyful: The Surprising Power of Ordinary Things to Create Extraordinary Happiness.* Little, Brown Spark, 2018.

Granneman, Jenn, and Andre Sólo. *Sensitive: The Hidden Power of the Highly Sensitive Person in a Loud, Fast, Too-much World.* Harmony Books, 2023.

Henderson, Donna, Sarah Wayland, and Jamell White. *Is This Autism? A Guide for Clinicians and Everyone Else.* Routledge, 2023.

Marlowe, Pasha. *Creating Cultures of Neuroinclusion: A Framework for Peopling and Engaging Diverse Talent.* Neurobelonging, 2024.

Maté, Gabor, MD. *When the Body Says No: The Cost of Hidden Stress.* Trade Paper Press, 2011.

Maté, Gabor, MD. *The Myth of Normal: Trauma, Illness and Healing in a Toxic Culture.* Avery, 2022.

Moorjani, Anita. *Sensitive is the New Strong: The Power of Empaths in an Increasingly Harsh World.* Atria/Enliven Books, 2021.

Nerenberg, Jenara. *Divergent Mind: Thriving in a World That Wasn't Designed for You.* HarperOne, 2020.

Praslova, Ludmila N. *The Canary Code: A Guide to Neurodiversity, Dignity, and Intersectional Belonging at Work.* Berrett-Koehler Publishers, 2024.

Podcasts

Ballantyne, Amy, host. Power To The People Pleasers. https://open.spotify.com/show/0pKHqV7ijb28bkHnQTupFj?si=55e5214ca4324670.

Bjelland, Julie, host. The Sensitive and Neurodivergent Podcast with Julie Bjelland. https://open.spotify.com/show/4NmbLzQqxuDp4Er7mNHWOh?si=09a698235cf94102.

Kumar, Clare, host. Happy Space Podcast. https://clarekumar.com/podcast/.

Websites

Aron, Elaine. The Highly Sensitive Person. https://hsperson.com/.

Bjelland, Julie. JulieBjelland.com. https://www.juliebjelland.com/.

Engelbrecht, Natalie. Embrace Autism: The Ultimate Autism Resource. https://embrace-autism.com/.

Jacobs Foundation. SensitivityResearch.com. https://sensitivityresearch.com/.

Neff, Megan Anna. Neurodivergent Insights. https://neurodivergentinsights.com/.

YouTube channels

Autistic Girls Network. https://www.youtube.com/@AutisticGirlsNetwork. A UK charity that "campaigns for earlier diagnosis/recognition of autism and offers support and resources to those identifying as autistic girls or non-binary young people and their families and to professionals."

Dr. Kim Sage. https://www.youtube.com/@DrKimSage/videos. Licensed clinical psychologist who shares content about late-diagnosed autism in high-masking women, along with videos on a range of mental health topics.

Mom on the Spectrum. https://www.youtube.com/@MomontheSpectrum. A late-diagnosed autistic woman who teaches "late-diagnosed autistic adults how to navigate life on the autism spectrum."

Purple Ella. https://www.youtube.com/@PurpleElla. Content from a late-diagnosed AuDHDer on autism, ADHD & neurodiversity.

Acknowledgments

I wrote my first book in elementary school. The little, handwritten book about a little bear's birthday party won a district award, of which I was very proud. Since then, I've thought about writing a "real" book many times: *Blind Dates from Hell* got some traction, until I lost everything on my computer and didn't have the heart to start over. I considered writing a comprehensive guide to moving for single women, and many people have asked for a book about my experiences living in eight other countries. That one might still happen someday.

This book wasn't planned. It was only when a publisher reached out and we had a couple of conversations about my work and why I care so deeply about it that I began to see it take shape and know it might make a difference. I owe thanks to Eric Koester for both the prompt and the title. *Perceptive* might not be in your hands now otherwise.

Writing essays and chapters comes fairly easily to me. A book, though, is a whole different animal. This was hard, and scary, for a lot of reasons I hadn't anticipated when I started the project. I'm thrilled that I did it, and deeply grateful for all the support I received from so many people on so many levels. I'm a little too used to doing things on my own. But a book can't be done that way; it truly takes a village.

Many thanks and hugs to all the highly perceptive women who shared their stories with me so I could share them with readers: Alecia Page, Amy Ballantyne, Amy Wilson, Clare Kumar, Esther Bergsma, Jemma Campbell, Kalen Cobb, Kara Peabody, Karen Renee Halseth, Kit Unger, Kristina Foge, Krystal Jones, Mindy Yang, Minette Norman, Mollie Isaacks, and Tricia Livermore. Your empathy, vulnerability, and authenticity made the collaboration an absolute pleasure and added value throughout the book and the journey. And a warm thank you to Jess Norris, who shared her experience with late-diagnosed ADHD with me over several conversations and inspired me to pursue my own diagnosis.

Bringing a book into the world isn't for the faint of heart—and it's not an inexpensive venture! Without the crowdfunding campaign that I hadn't realized I'd have to build, launch, and manage (a story for another time), *Perceptive* would still be a draft waiting to see the light of day. As if asking for help weren't hard enough, I had to ask everyone I'd ever known for money! This was way out of my comfort zone and an enormous learning experience. Special thanks to everyone who supported the campaign: Crystal Webber, Tetyana Colosivschi, Melinda Burrell, Erin Musgrave, Minette Norman, Agustin Soler, Krystal Jones, Doris Lee, Richard Hecht, Kristina Foge, Jodi Callahan, Nicholas Bernstein,

Dave Kerpen, Kara Peabody, Taylor LeCroy, Tom Bentley, Jemma Campbell, Jennifer Katan, Betty Dayron, Nicole Peterhans, Sanchit Gupta, Julie Mannheimer, Ted Radway, Quentin Finney, Debra Graugnard, Wrena D'Souza, Scot Copeland, Amy Pierquet, Kristen Wilkinson, Gina Shilhanek, Susan Korthase, Jessica Lindsey, Saray Gutierrez, Avis Yu, Michael Randel, Lisa Barnett, Dortha Hise, Rachel Kumar, Joe Lalley, Amy Luckey, Michael Rose, Jeff Jacobs, Saji Haratani, Tigana Lê, Cristina Stoll, Chanon Bernstein, Lisa Tracy, Barbara Greene, Wendy Wolffson, Audrey Donaldson, Lauran Star, Kristina Boylan, Tess Dixon, Samee Sheikh, Teri Swope, Lindsey Frederick, M'Elena Walker, Elaine Lin Hering, Katy Sullivan, Kit Unger, Nicholas Whitaker, Patty Laushman, Amy Ballantyne, Susan Gash, Andrew Brentano, Alecia Page, Josh Jacobs, Sheila McCarthy, Maria Pis-Lopez, Nat Chaitkin, Ghilaine Chan, Ellisha Tully, Ali Arena, Nicole Kim, Alexis Kraus, Takashi Fukuda, Sabrina Riley, Richard Bernstein, Sarah Marshall, Serene Mireles, Laïla von Alvensleben, Karen Renee Halseth, Arkady Vitrouk, Nidhi Gupta, Martin Drux, Julie Washburn, Brooke Stearns Lawson, Esther Bergsma, Grace Gellerman, Anna Tapp, Eric Koester, Kent & Patty Anker, Christine Martell, Scot Steele, Chirona Silverstein, Jenna Feldman, Lindsay Barnett, Jennifer Shaw Heller, Corrie Ratzat, Jen Marr, and Denisse Crapanzano.

Thank you, too, to everyone who supported the campaign by sharing it in your newsletters, podcasts and communities—Angilie Kapoor, Jay Fairbrother, Jennifer Hough, Shauna Van Mourik, Christene Sismondo, Melinda Meszaros, Mindy Yang and Stephanie Feuer, Jodi Callahan, Minette Norman, and many more. Everyone who got involved made a difference.

Early readers are critical, bringing different perspectives and highlighting gaps and areas where clarity or more explanation are needed. Maria Pis-Lopez, Kara Peabody, Kalen Cobb, Jemma Campbell, Ghilaine Chan, Francine Joselowsky, Niki Mathias, Jo Meadows, Craig Brooks, Rachel Kumar, Tess Dixon, Tom Bentley, Jodi Callahan, Esther Bergsma, Mollie Isaacks, and Katy Sullivan: I'm deeply grateful for your time, thoughtful input, and encouragement.

Thank you to the pros who helped shepherd *Perceptive* out into the world: Angela Ivey for cheering me on through the first draft and Stephanie McKibben for your patience and compassion throughout the (first, painful!) prelaunch phase; Becky Robinson, Amy Driehorst, Lori Weidert, Meredith Mix, and Keri Hales at Weaving Influence for the abundance of support in turning a manuscript into an actual book; and Rachel Royer for the beautiful cover and interior design.

Karen Renee, Kiki, Nicole P., Minette, Ghilaine, Tetyana, Mindy B., Jodi, Takashi, Grace, Amy L.—the chats, laughs, sanity checks, meals, virtual and physical hugs, and moral and emotional support got me through and kept my spirits up during the hardest parts. Joe Lalley—it was so helpful to talk with someone else who was doing all this at the same time! I'm looking forward to reading your book. Liz Heaney, thank you for giving me a place to stay in San Francisco when I desperately needed a change of scene, good food, and to see a few friends in person.

And finally, to my family: thank you and I love you.

About the author

Rachel Eve Radway has always known that she was wired a little differently. Despite being highly sensitive, an introvert and a natural nester, she's lived in nine countries and eight US states, and had almost as many careers. As a multipotentialite, lifelong learner and late-diagnosed AuDHDer, Rachel thrives on change and creates it when things get dull. After almost 30 years in the corporate world, she became a certified professional coach, and loves seeing her clients light up when they finally feel seen and understood.

Perceptive is Rachel's first full-length book. She's a contributing author to *Single State of the Union: Single Women Speak Out on Life, Love, and the Pursuit of Happiness* (Seal Press, 2007), and *Leading with Compassion: Cultivating Connection from the Inside Out* (Changing Work, 2025).

When she's not coaching, leading mastermind groups, mentoring, speaking, or writing, Rachel might be found reading, traveling, experimenting with various crafts, or exploring California's Central Coast, where she's currently based.

About RER Coaching

Before launching RER Coaching, Rachel Radway spent more than 25 years in tech startups, national nonprofits and Fortune 500s in a range of industries, with leadership roles in content strategy, communications, brand management, design operations and team ops. Her corporate experience inspired her dual mission: (1) helping leaders create the conditions they need to thrive personally and professionally, while (2) fostering inclusive workplace cultures where everyone feels safe, seen, valued and engaged.

Rachel's coaching work and mastermind programs empower and support high-achieving women who care deeply about their people and their purpose, value empathy and integrity, and promote organizational success over personal agendas. Read what her clients say about working with Rachel at https://www.rercoaching.com/testimonials.

RER Coaching offers 1:1 leadership and executive coaching and mentoring as well as small-group programs. Rachel also speaks to teams, employee resource groups and other organizations about high sensory perception, neurodiversity and inclusion.

Rachel received her coach training and certification from Erickson Coaching International, winner of the 2024 ICF Impact Award for Global Coaching Education Provider.

To connect with Rachel and RER Coaching:

- Follow her on LinkedIn at https://www.linkedin.com/in/reradway/.
- Visit rercoaching.com.
- Subscribe to the RER Coaching newsletter at http://eepurl.com/iEkf2s.
- Schedule a coaching discovery call at https://calendly.com/reradway/30-minute-discovery-call.
- To discuss booking a talk or custom workshop, email info@rercoaching.com.

www.ingramcontent.com/pod-product-compliance
Lightning Source LLC
Chambersburg PA
CBHW071213260425
25690CB00008B/28